THE COMPLETE POETI

Giacomo da Lentini

This volume presents the first translation in English of the complete poetry of Giacomo da Lentini, the first major lyric poet of the Italian vernacular. He was the leading exponent of the Sicilian School (c.1220–1270) as well as the inventor of the sonnet. Featuring illustrations and new English translations of some forty lyrics, Richard Lansing revives the work of a pioneer of Italian literature, a poet who helped pave the way for later writers such as Dante and Petrarch.

Giacomo da Lentini is hailed as the earliest poet to import the Occitan tradition of love poetry into the Italian vernacular. This edition of Giacomo fills a gap in the canon of translations of Italian literature in English and serves as a vital reference source for students as well as scholars and teachers interested in the literature of the romance languages.

(The Lorenzo da Ponte Italian Library)

GIACOMO DA LENTINI was an Italian poet of the thirteenth century and a member of the Sicilian School during the reign of Frederick II. The topics of his poetry primarily concerned courtly and chivalrous love.

RICHARD LANSING is a professor emeritus of Italian and Comparative Literature at Brandeis University.

AKASH KUMAR is visiting assistant professor of Literature at the University of California, Santa Cruz.

THE DA PONTE ITALIAN LIBRARY

Giacomo da Lentini

THE COMPLETE POETRY

Translation and Notes by Richard Lansing
Introduction by Akash Kumar

UNIVERSITY OF TORONTO PRESS
Toronto Buffalo London

© University of Toronto Press 2018
Toronto Buffalo London
utorontopress.com
Printed in the U.S.A.

ISBN 978-1-4875-0376-5 (cloth)   ISBN 978-1-4875-2286-5 (paper)

∞ Printed on acid-free, 100% post-consumer recycled paper with vegetable-based inks.

The Lorenzo Da Ponte Italian Library

Library and Archives Canada Cataloguing in Publication

Giacomo, da Lentini, active 13th century
[Poems. English]
The complete poetry of Giacomo Da Lentini / translation and notes
by Richard Lansing; introduction by Akash Kumar.

(The Da Ponte Italian library)
Includes bibliographical references and index.
ISBN 978-1-4875-0376-5 (cloth). – ISBN 978-1-4875-2286-5 (paper)

I. Lansing, Richard H., translator   II. Title.   III. Series: Lorenzo
da Ponte Italian library

PQ4471.G3A2 2018   851'.1   C2018-900232-8

This book has been published under the aegis of Agincourt Press LTD.

This book has been published with the financial assistance of a grant
provided by the Brandeis University Office of the Dean of the College
of Arts and Sciences.

University of Toronto Press acknowledges the financial assistance to its
publishing program of the Canada Council for the Arts and the Ontario
Arts Council, an agency of the Government of Ontario.

Canada Council
for the Arts

Conseil des Arts
du Canada

ONTARIO ARTS COUNCIL
CONSEIL DES ARTS DE L'ONTARIO
an Ontario government agency
un organisme du gouvernement de l'Ontario

Funded by the
Government
of Canada

Financé par le
gouvernement
du Canada

For
Camilla Wynne

Angelica figura e comprobata

Contents

Acknowledgments

I would like first to thank Christopher Kleinhenz for the many hours of stimulating conversation spent discussing the nuances of Il Notaro's poetry, for offering an abundance of sound advice, and, especially, for his generous comments as a reviewer for the University of Toronto Press. I am also grateful for the guidance and suggestions provided by the anonymous readers for the Press. My appreciation extends to Teodolinda Barolini for her unstinting support of the present project, to Guy Raffa for negotiating several twists and turns along the way, to Antonio Lanza for his philological insight, and to Roberto Antonelli for his encouragement in general, as well as for making available the Italian text of his critical edition of Giacomo da Lentini's poetry. My greatest personal debt, finally, is to Akash Kumar, who not only graciously accepted my invitation to provide an introduction to accompany my translation of the lyrics, but also selflessly engaged in many discussions aimed at resolving queries about Giacomo's use of rhetorical colors, the syntactic and semantic properties of his verse, and the conceptual intentionality of his lyric voice.

I wish also to convey my gratitude to the Brandeis University Office of the Dean of the College of Arts and Sciences for its generous support toward the publication of this book.

The illustrated manuscript anthology of 13th-century Italian poetry known as Banco Rari 217 is considered the oldest of the three principal sources that we have of the poetry of this period. Consequently, these select moments of transcription, or Tuscanized translations, of Giacomo's poetry might be considered some of the oldest that we still possess. The illustrator of this manuscript is notable for his minute attention to the text of the poems whose initial letter he illustrates.

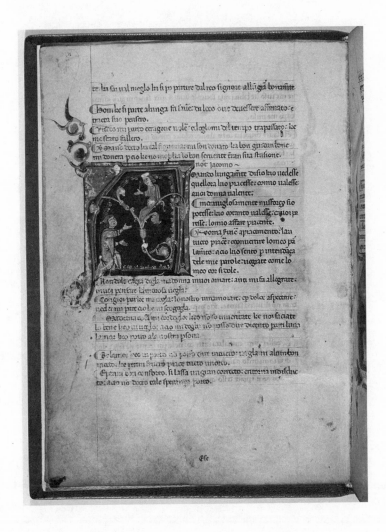

Figure 1. This manuscript page, with its evocative scene of a lover gesturing to his lady in a tree, contains Giacomo's canzone "Amando lungiamente." The illustrator is perhaps taking his cue from the fruit and orchard metaphor deployed in the third stanza of the poem. MS Banco Rari 217, 8v, Biblioteca Nazionale Centrale di Firenze

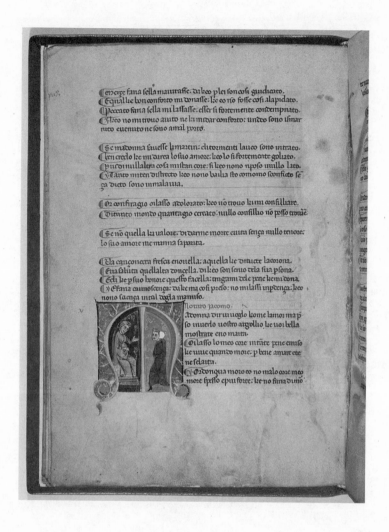

Figure 2. This page, with its historiated M creating a hierarchy between male lover and lady on high, contains Giacomo's celebrated poem "Madonna, dir vo voglio." MS Banco Rari 217, 21v, Biblioteca Nazionale Centrale di Firenze

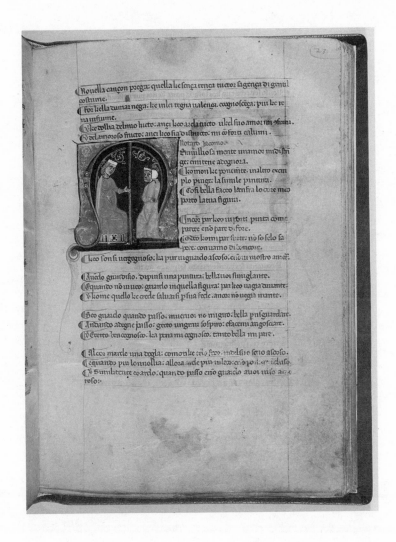

Figure 3. This page, containing a very similar historiated M to that of 21v, contains Giacomo's canzone "Meravigliosa-mente." MS Banco Rari 217, 23r, Biblioteca Nazionale Centrale di Firenze

THE COMPLETE POETRY

Giacomo da Lentini

Introduction

Some of the very earliest literary texts written in the Italian vernacular date from the early thirteenth century and take root in the court of emperor Frederick II in Palermo, Sicily. The finest and most important poet in his entourage was Giacomo da Lentini, the leading exponent of a group of poets that became known as the Sicilian "school" of poetry. He is regarded as the inventor of the sonnet, a poetic form known to have originated in Frederick's court and one with which Giacomo experimented extensively. Giacomo brought Occitan poetry – its forms, its themes, its conventions – to Italian shores, while his erudite use of images taken from the natural world and the philosophical underpinnings of his poetry exerted a significant degree of influence over the poets of his own and succeeding generations, which included a group known as the Stilnovist poets, whose most notable exponent was Dante Alighieri. Giacomo is unquestionably the first major lyric poet of the Italian vernacular whose presence looms large in any consideration of the history of Italian poetry. In light of the sonnet's distinction as a dominant form of lyric poetry in world literature, Giacomo's role takes on a still greater degree of importance.

While Giacomo da Lentini's status as inventor of the sonnet cannot be confirmed beyond all doubt, his sonnets, of which there are twenty-two of firm attribution, are by far the most numerous among those preserved of the earliest practitioners of the craft. Moreover, he demonstrates the greatest degree of technical variation in his handling of its formal properties.[1] The history of critical debate concerning the invention of the sonnet has tended to be divided between two theories: one claiming

---

1 For a recent and convincing case on Giacomo as the inventor of the form and his overarching influence in the establishment of the Italian lyric tradition, see Antonelli, "Giacomo da Lentini e l'invenzione della lirica italiana."

that it emerged from the Occitan model of the *canso* and particularly from the exchange of individual *coblas* (stanzas) among poets (known as a *tenso*), and the other that it was adapted from the Sicilian popular form of the *strambotto*. Seminal work by scholars such as Christopher Kleinhenz and Roberto Antonelli has succeeded in shifting the scales toward the Occitan hypothesis. As Kleinhenz observes, "the sonnet, as the only distinctive Italian verse form produced by the Sicilians, crowns the movement away from strict adherence to Provençal models by harmonizing traditional and new elements, according to a theory of poetics which we might term "imitative innovation" (33).[2] Such a model captures a key aspect of Giacomo's poetry as building on the tradition before him while simultaneously breaking new ground in a new vernacular setting. And as Gianfranco Folena contends, in arguing against the romantic notion of an arch-poet who singlehandedly begins a new literary tradition, the reality is not "in principio fuit poeta" ("in the beginning was the poet"), but rather "in principio fuit interpres" ("in the beginning was the interpreter").[3]

Giacomo, however, enjoyed a significant reception by the poetic tradition that followed in his wake. Indeed, we can speak of Giacomo as the founder of a school of poetry almost exclusively devoted to the topic of love. The most significant practitioners were Guido delle Colonne, generally regarded as the finest poet after Giacomo; Pier della Vigna, who served at the imperial court as Frederick II's secretary; Giacomino Pugliese, who in all probability composed the earliest canzone that we can date with certainty (c. 1230); Stefano Protonotaro, whose canzone *Pir meu cori alligrari* constitutes the only lyric of the School extant in its original Sicilian linguistic form; and Rinaldo d'Aquino, Mazzeo di Ricco, as well as Frederick himself. Giacomo's followers were not limited to the geographical proximity of the island of Sicily alone. Both Percivalle Doria, a Genovese military leader, and Re Enzo, a son of Frederick who resided in Bologna, define the School's extended reach into northern Italy. Since Frederick's royal court was peripatetic in nature, moving itinerantly from location to location, the School's influence naturally spread throughout the Italian-speaking territories under the emperor's control.

---

2 Kleinhenz, *The Early Italian Sonnet*. This study remains the most complete and influential anglophone treatment of the poetry of Giacomo da Lentini.

3 Folena, *Volgarizzare e tradurre*. The relationship between vernacular invention and translation has been an important current of recent scholarship. See, especially, Cornish, *Vernacular Translation in Dante's Italy*.

In all, the repertory of the School comprises about 150 lyrics, of which one-fifth remain anonymous, composed by twenty-five poets.[4]

Of the three principal Tuscan anthologies that preserve the Italian vernacular lyrics of the thirteenth century, by far the most sizable is the Vaticano Latino 3793, dated to the late thirteenth to early fourteenth centuries and containing some 1,000 lyric components.[5] It is notable both that Giacomo's poetry opens this anthology – with his canzone *Madonna, dir vo voglio* – and that the section of sonnets begins with Giacomo's poetic exchange (known as a *tenzone*) with the Abate di Tivoli. For the compilers and scribes of the VL 3793, consequently, there is no question of Giacomo's poetic preeminence and his status as principal poet of the Scuola Siciliana.

The preservation of Giacomo's poetry in these Tuscan anthologies brings out two key facts regarding his poetry. First, his poetic corpus is the most extensively preserved of the early Sicilian poets, far outnumbering that of any other poet associated with Frederick's court. And second, we do not possess the original form of his poetry – or, indeed, almost any of the original poetry of the Sicilian school – but rather versions that were Tuscanized to varying degrees by the scribes and compilers of these lyric anthologies.

With respect to the material transmission of his lyric, Giacomo emerges as a dominant figure. His status as poetic authority also emerges from within his corpus, particularly in his two exchanges with other poets. In the exchange with the Abate di Tivoli, Giacomo takes a fellow poet to task for his conception that love can exist as an independent entity. He extends his critique to all those who share such a view: "Per ch'io vi saccia dir lo convenente / di quelli che del trovar non ànno posa / ca dicono in lor ditto spessamente / ch'amore à in sé deïtate inclosa" (So you may grasp the view of those / Who never cease to write of love / And often claim in poetry / That love contains divinity) (*Feruto sono isvarïatamente*, 18b.3–6). Although initially the Abate resists Giacomo's view, he concludes the exchange with an admission of defeat: "Con vostro onore facciovi uno 'nvito / ser Giacomo valente, a cui inchino" (To honor you I send you this appeal, / My worthy Giacomo, to whom I bow) (*Con vostro*

---

4 Luigina Morini in Segre and Ossola, *Antologia della poesia italiana*, 29.

5 The other two anthologies are Laurenziano Rediano 9 and Banco Rari 217 (formerly known as Palatino 418). Of particular note are the recent facsimiles of these manuscripts published by SISMEL, along with a fourth volume of critical overviews and interventions. See Leonardi, *I canzonieri*.

onore, 18e.1–2). In the other *tenzone* on the nature of love in which he participates, along with Iacopo Mostacci and Pier della Vigna, Giacomo censures and corrects his fellow court poets. His sonnet *Amor è uno disio che ven da core* marks the third and final word on the matter. It provides an assertive, physiological definition of love that will come to influence later generations of love poets. The two exchanges establish the parameters of Giacomo's contemporary influence, the second *tenzone* by reinforcing his position within the Federician court and the first by establishing the reach of his lyric beyond the geographical boundaries of Sicily, much in the manner of the emperor's political reach and the nature of his peripatetic court.

We know very little about the events of Giacomo da Lentini's personal life. He was born at the turn of the thirteenth century into a noble family of Lentini, a small town that lies halfway between Catania and Syracuse just inland from the eastern shores of Sicily. His professional activity as notary in the court of Frederick II is substantiated by official documents dated to 1233 and 1240.[6] Both Giacomo's personal origin and professional identity find expression in his poetry. In the closing verses of the canzone *Meravigliosa-mente*, the poet publicizes his identity: "Lo vostro amor, ch'è caro, / donatelo al notaro / ch'è nato da Lentino" (Your love, which is so dear, / Vouchsafe the Notary / A native of Lentini) (2.61–3). The identification of Giacomo with his professional title persists in the manuscript tradition as well. In the case of *Meravigliosa-mente*, each of the three major anthologies contain the poem and identify its author with a rubric above: the Vaticano Latino 3793 attributes it to "Notaro giacommo," the Laurenziano Rediano 9 to "N. Jacomo," and the Banco Rari 217 to "Notaro Jacomo." The conflation of the poet's name and his court title is so complete that Dante refers to Giacomo only as the "Notaro" when he crafts a moment of literary history through an encounter with the Tuscan poet Bonagiunta Orbicciani in *Purgatorio* 24. Dante has Bonagiunta not only lay out an abbreviated history of the early lyric tradition, but also acknowledge and christen the "sweet new style" (*dolce stil novo*) as practiced by Dante and his fellow poets: "O frate issa vegg'io," diss'elli, "il nodo / che 'l Notaro e Guittone e me ritenne / di qua dal dolce stil novo ch'i' odo!" ("O brother, now I see," he said, "the knot that kept the Notary, Guittone, and me

---

6 On the topic of Giacomo's family as well as the official documents prepared by him, see Sciascia, "Lentini e i Lentini dai Normanni al Vespro."

short of the sweet new manner that I hear) (*Purgatorio* 24.55–7).[7] Though the point here is the establishing of difference between the lyric past and Dante's lofty present, we might also consider the idea of fellowship that is implicit in the term *frate* (brother), a term more pointed here perhaps than in its generic use for all purgatorial brethren. Most tellingly, it is Giacomo who is named first in this lyric genealogy and thus accorded the prime position of the founding father of Italian poetry.

There has been strong surge of recent interest in the Italian poetry of the thirteenth century. The new edition of the poetry of the Sicilian school, *I poeti della scuola siciliana* (Mondadori, 2008), foregrounds not only Giacomo da Lentini (vol. 1) and the other poets of the Federician court (vol. 2), but also the Siculo-Tuscans (vol. 3), who constitute the next step in the migration of Italian poetry into Tuscany. Even more recently, Aldo Menichetti has published a new critical edition of the poetry of Bonagiunta Orbicciani (c. 1226–96), the same Bonagiunta Dante has speak in *Purgatorio* 24,[8] and Antonello Borra has just published a select translation of the poetry and epistolary production of Guittone d'Arezzo (c. 1235–94), considered the principal Tuscan poet immediately following the Sicilians.[9] Taken together, these volumes attest to a renewed interest in early Italian poetry and reflect a holistic critical approach rather than one that relies on inherited taxonomies that began with Dante's influential role as a literary historian.

Giacomo's own influential role must be seen as a direct product of the cultural sponsorship of Frederick II (1194–1250), who was dubbed *stupor mundi*, wonder of the world, on the basis of his numerous extraordinary accomplishments as ruler, writer, and patron of the sciences and the arts. The Federician court was a hotbed of intellectual activity and intercultural exchange, and it is abundantly clear that Frederick II invested much in the promotion of intellectual inquiry and artistic production. Frederick himself wrote lyric poetry, testifying to his personal commitment to the establishment of a new vernacular art. Even a scholar such as David Abulafia, who argues against the overblown image of Frederick II as *stupor mundi*, nonetheless concedes that "at the very highest rung of the intellectual ladder there were scholars of all three religions [Christian, Judaic, Muslim] who were willing to confront together problems

---

7 See Dante Alighieri, *Purgatory*, trans. Allen Mandelbaum (New York: Bantam, 1983). All subsequent citations of the *Purgatory* are to this edition.

8 Bonagiunta Orbicciani da Lucca, *Rime*.

9 Guittone d'Arezzo, *Selected Poems and Prose*.

they shared, in science or even religion, such as the proof of God's existence or the eternity of matter" (256–7).[10] The presence of figures such as the mathematician Leonardo Fibonacci and the astrologer and translator of Aristotle Michael Scot attests to the wealth of ideas, intellectual developments and innovations accessible to a court functionary and poet such as Giacomo da Lentini, whose lyric production epitomizes such an engagement.[11] These particular examples speak to the multicultural nature of knowledge production in the Federician court. While at court, Scot translated the Muslim philosopher Avicenna's commentary on Aristotle's *De animalibus* into Latin. Fibonacci introduced the Indian-Arabic numerical system to the West in his seminal work *Liber abaci*, drawing on both Latin and Arabic sources.[12] Each of these textual encounters places the poetry of Giacomo da Lentini within an important cultural context: Avicenna's commentary adds to our understanding of Giacomo's varied poetic bestiary (including salamanders, lions, vipers, and moths), and mathematical currents of the day reveal a relationship with the meter of the sonnet, as Wilhelm Pötters has shown.[13]

Translation, broadly speaking, lies at the heart of Giacomo's poetry. He borrows and adapts much of his formal poetic structures from the Occitan poetic tradition before him. Metrically speaking, Giacomo's canzoni and his sole *discordo* are adaptations, as the linguistic closeness of the words implies, of the Occitan forms of the *canso* and the *descort*. The sonnet's form radically distinguishes Giacomo's poetry from that of his predecessors in Provence, standing as a testament to his vernacular innovation. On the other hand, the exchange of sonnets with other poets replicates the Occitan *tenso*. Giacomo, moreover, translates many of the lyric tropes and courtly language from the Occitan tradition. The canzone *Guiderdone aspetto avere*, for example, begins with the word *guiderdone*, which translates *guerdon*, the conventional term in Occitan to denote the courtly lover's expected recompense for having served his lady. We are confronted with an even more

---

10 Abulafia, *Frederick II*. A useful recent assessment of the historical facts and subsequent development of the myths surrounding Frederick is Fulvio Delle Donne, *Federico II*.

11 For an interdisciplinary overview of cultural life at Frederick's court, see *Intellectual Life at the Court of Frederick II Hohenstaufen*. See also *Federico II e le nuove culture*.

12 On Michael Scot and his influence on Frederick II, see Morpurgo, "*Philosophia naturalis.*" On Leonardo Fibonacci's relationship to Arab mathematics, see Rashed, "Fibonacci e les mathématiques arabes."

13 Pötters, *Nascità del sonetto*.

explicit moment of translation in the canzone *Madonna, dir vo voglio*, in which Giacomo translates the entire first two stanzas of Occitan poet Folquet de Marselha's *canso A vos, midontç, voill retrair' en cantan*, as was first observed by the scholar Francesco Torraca.[14] But Giacomo does not merely turn one form of vernacular poetry into another; he works to create greater logical coherence in his canzone, transforms Folquet's recourse to a philosophical principle into a zoological example from the natural world, and moves beyond the bounds of Folquet's poem by adding three additional stanzas.[15]

Giacomo's poetry also reflects the influence of Andreas Capellanus's twelfth-century treatise *De amore*, which provides a theoretical basis for many of the positions on love advanced by the Notaro. A good example is Giacomo's insistence on the primacy of love that is born from direct vision in the sonnet *Amor è uno disio che ven da lo core*. Other compelling intertexts include the French romance tradition, as seen in the direct reference to the story of Tristan and Isolde in the discord *Dal cor mi vene*: "bell'ò provato / mal che non salda: / Tristano Isalda / non amau sì forte" (I've borne a wound / That never heals: / Sir Tristan did not love / Isolde with such zeal) (5.37–40).[16] In a fusion of vernacular and classical culture, Ovid's *Ars amatoria* serves as another source of topoi for Giacomo's conception of love. The concluding lines of the sonnet *Sì come il sol che manda la sua spera* seem directly indebted to Ovid: "e due cori insemora li giunge, / de l'arte de l'amore sì gli aprende, / e face l'uno e l'altro d'amor pare" (And it joins two hearts into one / And teaches them the art of love: / Each loves the other equally) (21.12–14). Ovid's *Ars* becomes Giacomo's *arte* in a distillation of classical thought for a new vernacular audience.

While the end of the sonnet *Sì come il sol* features a recourse to Ovid, the bulk of the poem likens the behaviour of sunlight to the nature of love. A turn to the natural world denotes one of the hallmarks of Giacomo's poetry, borne out by his use of complex similes to depict the

---

14 See Torraca, "A proposito di Folchetto."
15 For more on this line of reasoning, see Michelangelo Picone, "Aspetti della tradizione/traduzione nei poeti siciliani," in Picone, *Percorsi della lirica duecentesca*.
16 While this reference speaks to a general storehouse of Arthurian romance in the Italian tradition, Roberto Antonelli also makes a compelling case for the specific influence of Thomas's *Tristan* in this particular verse. See Antonelli, *I poeti della Scuola siciliana*, vol. 1.

poet's amorous state. From the salamander's ability to reside in fire in *Madonna, dir vo voglio* to the value of precious stones in the sonnet *Diamante né smiraldo né zafino*, Giacomo continually draws upon a wide array of imagery that extends beyond the relationship between lover and beloved to touch on the world at large. One sonnet that captures well Giacomo's distillation of natural philosophy in his love lyric is *A l'aire claro ò vista ploggia dare*. The series of oxymoronic images that opens the sonnet might well be drawn from a nexus of natural philosophy current in Giacomo's day:

> A l'aire claro ò vista ploggia dare
> ed a lo scuro rendere clarore;
> e foco arzente ghiaccia diventare,
> e freda neve rendere calore.

> On clear days I have seen it rain
> And I've seen darkness flash with light
> And likewise lightning turn to hail
> And freezing snow engender heat.   (26.1–4)

While the initial images are of a quotidian and familiar sort – indeed it can rain on a clear day and the darkness of night regularly does fill with light – the succeeding lines expand to a more complicated meteorological assimilation. How might burning fire turn into ice, or cold snow produce heat? These lines might well allude to the belief that hail was produced out of lightning and that the process of crystallizing (freezing) generated heat from snow by means of reflecting sunlight, concepts common to the science of the day.

Attention to scientific principles becomes more theoretical in form in a sonnet like *Or come pote sì gran donna entrare*, where optical theory is marshaled to consider how large objects can possibly enter the eyes. And in the sonnet *Sì come il sol manda che la sua spera*, the poet similarly likens the dart of love passing through the lover's eyes to light passing through glass without physically breaking it. Such metaphors and scientific considerations will continue to find currency in the further development of the Italian lyric, from Dante to Galileo.

Though he borrows heavily from the Occitan tradition, Giacomo also raises the bar by intensifying the tension between secular and sacred desires. In sonnet 27, *Io m'aggio posto in core a Dio servire*, Giacomo claims to serve God so that he might eventually find a place for himself in paradise, then boldly exclaims that he would not wish to go there if it meant separation from his lady love.

Io m'aggio posto in core a Dio servire,
com'io potesse gire in paradiso,
al santo loco ch'aggio audito dire
o' si mantien solazzo, gioco e riso.
Sanza mia donna non vi voria gire,
quella ch'à blonda testa e claro viso,
che sanza lei non poteria gaudere,
estando da la mia donna diviso.

Ma non lo dico a tale intendimento
perch'io pecato ci vellesse fare,
se non veder lo suo bel portamento
e lo bel viso e 'l morbido sguardare:
che 'l mi teria in gran consolamento,
veggendo la mia donna in ghiora stare.

I've set my heart on serving God
So I might go to Paradise,
That holy place, as I have heard,
Where all is laughter, fun, and games.
I would not go without my love,
Whose face is bright and hair is blond,
For without her I'd have no joy,
Deprived of her companionship.

Yet I do not intend for this
To signify I wish to sin,
But just to see her gracious mien,
Her lovely face, and kind regard:
For it would bring me great delight
To see my love in glory's realm.

The tension is left unresolved in the tercets of the sonnet (9–14), with Giacomo pulling back and claiming that he does not intend to transgress a religious boundary in what he says. His wish to look on his lady in a state of glory – "veggendo la mia donna in ghiora stare" (to see my love in glory's realm) (14) – sows a seed that will prove to be very influential for Stilnovist poets who equate love of woman with love of the divine, beginning with Guido Guinizzelli and culminating with Dante's idealization of Beatrice.[17]

Giacomo's radical experiments with the nascent vernacular find an apt reception in the consummate poetry of the *Commedia*. One significant point of contact occurs with the use of the Latin term *quia*. When the Abate di Tivoli addresses the god of love as a separate entity in an exchange sonnet, Giacomo seeks to correct him on the basis of Scholastic argumentation, playing upon the Abate's religious vocation: "E chi lo mi volesse contastare, / io lo mostreria per *quia* e quanto, / come non è più d'una deïtate" (Should someone wish to quarrel with me / I'll demonstrate the reason why / There can be but one deity) (*Feruto sono*, 18b.9–11). Giacomo blends philosophical Latin with the new vernacular to wittily chastise his fellow poet and assert his own authority by using terms taken from his adversary's professional vocabulary. We do not come across another use of the word *quia* in the poetic tradition until *Purgatorio* 3, where Virgilio employs it to poignantly characterize the limits of human reason: "State contenti, umana gente, al *quia*; / ché se potuto aveste veder tutto, / mestier non era parturir Maria" (Confine yourselves, o humans, to the *quia*; / had you been able to see all, there would have been / no need for Mary to give birth) (*Purgatorio* 3.37–9). For both poets, the Scholastic term represents the extreme limit of human reason, all that can be known and done in language, although it takes on a bittersweet quality in the vision of the *Commedia*.

This kind of attention to the language of logic permeates Giacomo's poetry. In the sonnet *Sì alta amanza*, Giacomo deploys a logical turn-of-phrase at the precise point of the sonnet's formal turn, the *volta* (turn) that divides the octave and the sextet: "Donqua, madonna, se lacrime e pianto / de lo diamante frange le durezze, / vostre altezze poria isbasare / lo meo penar amoroso ch'è tanto" (So, Lady, if my tears and plaint / Can crack the diamond's stoniness, / The pain of love that burdens me / Might moderate your arrogance) (30.9–12). Such examples abound in Giacomo's poetry, attesting to a concerted effort on the part of the poet to create logical coherence amid the turmoil of amorous suffering and thus fuse philosophical method with the new form of vernacular poetry.

It is a critical commonplace that the Sicilian beginnings of the Italian lyric tradition are marked by a monotonous uniformity of theme: the

---

17 For an elegant appraisal of Dante's relationship to Giacomo and the preceding lyric tradition, see Barolini, "Dante and the lyric past."

poems seem to be about love and little else. But this is not the case with Giacomo. His full lyric corpus tells more than a love story. It reveals a poet who blends historical references with philosophical notions, and ethical principles with amatory praise. The canzone *Guiderdone aspetto avere* presents a lesson in economics at the level of simile. The poet does not despair at his lady's cruelty because he knows that a poor man can become rich with the right investment, one that he intends to make: "ca spesse volte vidi, – ed è provato / omo di poco affare / pervenire in gran loco: / se lo sape avanzare, / moltiplicar lo poco – ch'à 'quistato" (For often I have seen, as is well known, / A man of modest means / Attain a lofty rank, / If he improves his worth / By multiplying what he has acquired] (3.10–14). Further on, the beautiful yet unsympathetic lady is likened to a rich miser who risks becoming an outcast if he does not share his wealth: "com'omo ch'à richezze / ed usa scarsitade – di ciò ch'àve; / se non è bene-apreso, / nodruto e insegnato, / da ogn'omo 'nd'è ripreso, / orruto e dispregiato – e posto a grave" (Is like a man of wealth / Who's parsimonious with what he has; / If he is not well-bred, / Refined and well informed, / He'll be reproached by all, / Reviled, despised and put in dire straits) (3.37–42). A similar kind of ethical reasoning informs Giacomo's friendship sonnet *Quand'om à un bon amico leiale* (*When someone has a true and loyal friend*), which exhorts keeping true friends through proper courtly behaviour and censures treating friends as commodities. Usually left out of poetic anthologies, the sonnet is unusual for the fact that it does not speak of amatory love at all. Indeed, the word for "love" never appears.

Though much of Giacomo's love lyrics remain firmly entrenched in the non-specific, there are several instances of historical specificity that lend his poetry a concreteness. While his self-identification as the Notary born in Lentini at the close of *Meravigliosa-mente* grounds Giacomo's poetry in his native soil, a moment of geographical firmness in the canzone *Dolce coninzamento* looks outward from the island to the peninsula. He does not just say that he sings of his love for the most beautiful lady, but tellingly plays upon the political geography of the 'other' Sicily, that extends outward to Naples as part of Frederick's political reach: "Dolce coninzamento / canto per la più fina / che sia, al mio parimento, / d'Agri infino in Mesina" (I sing a sweet preamble / For the best of all, / Or so she seems to me, / I mean the loveliest, / From Agri to Messina) (17.1–4). This range, from Messina to the river Agri in Basilicata, might well echo Giacomo's travels there in his role as court functionary. More striking still is Giacomo's singular moment of political propaganda in the canzone *Ben m'è venuto prima cordoglienza*. To convey his lady's extraordinary degree of pride, Giacomo crafts a comparison based on the political characteristics of several central and northern Italian cities:

E voi che sete senza percepenza,
como Florenza – che d'orgoglio sente,
guardate a Pisa di gran canoscenza,
che teme tenza – d'orgogliosa gente:
sì lungiamente – orgoglio m'à in bailia,
Melano del carroccio par che sia

And you who lack a penetrating eye,
Like Florence, which behaves with arrogance,
Direct your eyes on Pisa, ever wise,
Which fears a feud with people who are proud:
For quite some time your pride has mastered me,
You're like Milan with its war chariot.   (7.33–8)

The attack on Florence for its excessive pride (i.e., its Guelf opposition to the emperor) and the praise of Pisa's prudence in allying itself with Frederick allow for a tentative dating of this sonnet to 1234, when Frederick II found himself beleaguered by such a political situation. The mention of Milan's *carroccio*, or war chariot, may be a generic point of reference, but could also refer to Frederick's taking of the *carroccio* in the 1237 battle of Cortenuova. The clarity of the historical reference is an unusual feature for a love poet such as Giacomo.

This marks the first translation in English of the complete set of Giacomo da Lentini's poems. Previously, renderings of only several of his most celebrated canzoni and sonnets have appeared together in one place, and it is nothing short of surprising that Giacomo's corpus of verse has until now not received greater attention by translators. The present translation of all forty-one lyrics offers readers access for the first time in the English language to the full range of Giacomo's creative inventiveness as a master of rhetorical devices and modes of emotional expressivity. Like his recent sprightly translations of Dante's lyric poetry that accompany commentary by Teodolinda Barolini in *Dante's Lyric Poetry: Poems of Youth and of the* Vita Nuova (University of Toronto Press, 2014), Richard Lansing's versions are presented as poems in their own right that seek to balance the competing claims of a text's poetic musicality and fidelity to its conceptual expressions.

There is a limited history of English engagement with Giacomo da Lentini's poetry. The Pre-Raphaelite poet Dante Gabriel Rossetti, in his 1861 anthology of translations of early Italian poetry before Dante, had this to say about Giacomo:

> The low estimate expressed of him as well as of Bonaggiunta and Guittone, by Dante (Purg. C.xxiv) must be understood as referring in great measure to their want of grammatical purity and nobility of style, as we may judge when the passage is taken in conjunction with the principles of the *De Vulgari Eloquio* ... A translation does not suffer from such offences of dialect as may exist in its original.[18]

Rossetti falls prey to a prejudice that tells us a great deal about how successful Dante has been in determining not only his own reception but also that of the poets before him. And here we have Rossetti weighing in on the vexed question of poetic translation, casting himself in the role of redeemer and purifier of language by speaking of Giacomo's "offences of dialect" that could be corrected, as it were, in translation. Rossetti, however, never follows through with a complete 'correction,' translating in the end merely seven lyric components, a mix of three sonnets and four *canzoni*. Frede Jensen's 1986 anthology, *The Poetry of the Sicilian School*, brought the total to ten components (six *canzoni* and four sonnets).[19] All this from a body of sixteen *canzoni*, twenty-two sonnets, and a *discordo* that Italian editors have firmly attributed to the poet.[20]

Such meagre attention to the poet over so long a period of time since Rossetti is fairly surprising, if only because Giacomo has long deserved far greater consideration as the putative inventor of the sonnet, a poetic form that has served as a model of imitation, technical innovation, and creative inspiration around the world for the past eight hundred years, from Shakespeare to Rabindranath Tagore. Instead, Giacomo is almost a forgotten voice. A major anthology of sonnets published only ten years

---

18 Rossetti, *The Early Italian Poets*, 8.
19 *The Poetry of the Sicilian School*, ed. and trans. Frede Jensen.
20 Citations are to Roberto Antonelli's most recent critical edition of Giacomo's poetry in *I poeti della Scuola siciliana*, vol. 1. Ernest Felix Langley's 1915 critical edition of Giacomo's work (with text in Italian only) represents an important moment of American scholarly engagement with the Sicilian poet and served as a reference point for twentieth-century Italian editors. See his *The Poetry of Giacomo da Lentino*.

ago, purporting to be an exploration of the sonnet through the centuries, barely alludes to its Sicilian origins and nowhere even mentions the name of Giacomo da Lentini.[21]

When Giacomo reached the end of his innovative translation of Folquet de Marselha's *canso* and was about to step out into the empty space of vernacular invention, he expressed a hint of hesitation: "vivo 'n foc'amoroso / e non saccio ch'eo dica: / lo meo lavoro spica – e non ingrana" (I live in passion's fire / Yet can't express just how. / My wheat sprouts ears, and yet no seed takes root) (*Madonna, dir vo voglio*, 1.31–2). Giacomo's hesitation is a signature moment, highlighting the difficulty and uncertainty inherent in his groundbreaking act of poetic creation. Kernels of poetry rarely produce transformative crops, but his seeds have indeed provided a great yield for the Italian poetic tradition and beyond. This new soil should show just how "ingranato" Giacomo da Lentini is in the world of poetry.

Akash Kumar
University of California at Santa Cruz

---

21 See Hirsch and Boland, *The Making of the Sonnet*. Dante and Petrarch are both featured, Dante being incorrectly singled out as "the first major practitioner of the sonnet form" (296).

The Canzoni and Discordo

1   Canzone

Madonna, dir vo voglio
como l'amor m'à priso,
inver' lo grande orgoglio
che voi, bella, mostrate, e no m'aita.
Oi lasso, lo meo core,   5
che 'n tante pene è miso
che vive quando more
per bene amare, e teneselo a vita!
Dunque mor' e viv'eo?
No, ma lo core meo   10
more più spesso e forte
che no faria di morte – naturale,
per voi, donna, cui ama,
più che se stesso brama,
e voi pur lo sdegnate: 15
amor, vostra 'mistate – vidi male.

Lo meo 'namoramento
non pò parire in detto,
ma sì com'eo lo sento
cor no lo penseria né diria lingua;   20
e zo ch'eo dico è nente
inver' ch'eo son distretto
tanto coralemente:
foc'aio al cor non credo mai si stingua;
anzi si pur alluma: 25
perché non mi consuma?
La salamandra audivi
che 'nfra lo foco vivi – stando sana;
eo sì fo per long'uso,
vivo 'n foc'amoroso   30
e non saccio ch'eo dica:
lo meo lavoro spica – e non ingrana.

1

My lady, I wish to tell you
How love has mastered me
Concerning the disdain
You show, my fair, and how he's of no help.
Alas, my weary heart   5
Now has so many wounds
That as it lives it dies
From loving well, and thinks of death as life.
Then I both die and live?
Not so, but my heart dies   10
More oft and painfully
Than it would if its death were natural,
Because of you, my fair,
Whom it loves and desires more than itself,
Though you keep spurning it: 15
My love, in loving you I am deceived.

The nature of my love
Cannot be put in words,
For what it feels like now
My heart cannot conceive nor tongue express;   20
And what I say is nil
Concerning the distress
I feel inside my heart.
I think the fire within will not die out,
But if it's still ablaze,   25
Why am I not consumed?
The salamander, I have heard,
Can live in fire and yet remain unharmed.
I've long endured like this,
I live in passion's fire,   30
Yet can't express just how.
My wheat sprouts ears, and yet no seed takes root.

Madonna, sì m'avene
ch'eo non posso avenire
com'eo dicesse bene   35
la propia cosa ch'eo sento d'amore:
sì com'omo in prudito
lo cor mi fa sentire,
che giamai no 'nd'è quito
mentre non pò toccar lo suo sentore.   40
Lo non-poter mi turba,
com'on che pinge e sturba,
e pure li dispiace
lo pingere che face, – e sé riprende,
che non fa per natura   45
la propïa pintura;
e non è da blasmare
omo che cade in mare – a che s'aprende.

Lo vostr'amor che m'àve
in mare tempestoso,   50
è sì como la nave
c'a la fortuna getta ogni pesanti,
e campan per lo getto
di loco periglioso:
similemente eo getto   55
a voi, bella, li mei sospiri e pianti,
che s'eo no li gittasse
parria che soffondasse,
e bene soffondara,
lo cor tanto gravara – in suo disio;   60
che tanto frange a terra
tempesta che s'aterra,
ed eo così rinfrango:
quando sospiro e piango – posar crio.

It comes to pass, my love,
That I cannot succeed
In putting into words   35
The very quality of love I feel;
My heart prompts me to feel
Like one who has an itch
And never gains relief
As long as he can't scratch the spot itself.   40
My lack distresses me,
Like one who paints, then rubs it off,
And yet still finds unfit
The picture that he paints, and blames himself
For failing to depict   45
An image perfectly;
Still one should not bear blame
For what one grabs when falling in the sea.

My love for you, which places me
Upon a stormy sea,   50
Is like a ship in peril
That must cast all its cargo overboard
And by that act all hands
Escape calamity;
Just so I cast to you,   55
My fair, my sighs and cries of agony.
If they weren't cast away
I think that I would sink,
And surely I would sink,
So much my yearning heart would weigh me down.   60
For as it comes ashore
A storm will break apart,
And likewise I break up:
Through tears and sighs, I seem to find some peace.

Assai mi son mostrato   65
a voi, bella spietata,
com'eo so' innamorato,
ma creio ch'e' dispiacerï' a voi pinto.
Poi ch'a me solo, lasso,
cotal ventura è data,   70
perché no mi 'nde lasso?
Non posso, di tal guisa Amor m'à vinto.
Vorria ch'or avenisse
che lo meo core 'scisse
come 'ncarnato tutto,   75
e non facesse motto – a voi, sdegnosa;
ch'Amore a tal l'adusse
ca, se vipera i fusse,
natura perderia:
a tal lo vederia, – fora pietosa.   80

I've shown abundantly   65
To you, dear heartless one,
How much I am in love,
But I think you'd dislike my portrait too.
Since such a fate as this
Is dealt to me alone,   70
Why do I not give up?
I lack the power, for Love has conquered me.
I wish it came to pass
My heart could come to life
Just like a human being   75
And spoke no word to you, disdainful one.
For Love has so degraded it
That if an asp were there,
It'd lose its inborn cruelty:
To see the heart like that, it would feel pity.   80

2   Canzonetta

Meravigliosa-mente
un amor mi distringe
e soven ad ogn'ora.
Com'omo che ten mente
in altro exemplo pinge   5
la simile pintura,
così, bella, facc'eo,
che 'nfra lo core meo
porto la tua figura.

In cor par ch'eo vi porti   10
pinta como parete,
e non pare di fore;
o Deo, co' mi par forte
non so se vi savete,
com' v'amo di bon core,   15
ca son sì vergognoso
ca pur vi guardo ascoso,
e non vi mostro amore.

Avendo gran disio
dipinsi una pintura,   20
bella, voi simigliante,
e quando voi non vio
guardo 'n quella figura
e par ch'eo v'aggia avante:
sì com'om che si crede   25
salvare per sua fede,
ancor non via davante.

Al cor m'ard'una doglia,
com'om che te·lo foco
a lo suo seno ascoso,   30
e quando più lo 'nvoglia,
tanto arde più loco

2

Extraordinarily
A love now grips me fast
And always rules my thoughts.
As one who gazes at
A model with great care   5
Can paint its replica,
So too, my love, can I,
For in my heart I bear
The image of your form.

I seem to bear you in my heart,   10
Portrayed as you appear,
Which can't be seen outside.
O God, how cruel it seems,
I don't know if you know
How truly I love you,   15
For I'm so timorous
I watch you secretly
And don't show you my love.

Possessed of great desire,
I painted, fairest one,   20
A picture of your likeness,
And when I don't see you,
I look upon that form
And think I have you here,
Like someone who believes   25
He'll save his soul through faith,
Though it's not there to see.

A torment sears my heart,
Like one who has a fire
Concealed within his breast: 30
The more he keeps it veiled
The more it burns apace

e non pò stare incluso:
similemente eo ardo
quando pass'e non guardo   35
a voi, vis'amoroso.

S'eo guardo quando passo,
inver' voi no mi giro,
bella, per risguardare;
andando ad ogni passo   40
sì getto uno sospiro
che facemi ancosciare;
e certo bene ancoscio,
ch'a pena mi conoscio,
tanto bella mi pare.   45

Assai v'aggio laudato,
madonna, in tutte parti
di bellezze ch'avete.
Non so se v'è contato
ch'eo lo faccia per arti,   50
che voi ve ne dolete:
sacciatelo per singa
zo ch'e' voi dire' a linga,
quando voi mi vedite.

Canzonetta novella,   55
và canta nova cosa;
lèvati da maitino
davanti a la più bella,
fiore d'ogn'amorosa,
bionda più ch'auro fino: 60
"Lo vostro amor, ch'è caro,
donatelo al notaro
ch'è nato da Lentino."

And cannot be contained:
Just so I burn when I
Pass by and do not gaze   35
At you, your pleasing face.

When passing, if I look,
I will not turn toward you,
My fair, to cast a glance.
With every step I take   40
I heave a mournful sigh
That leaves me in distress;
Indeed I weep so much
I scarcely know myself,
So beautiful you look.   45

I've praised abundantly,
My fair, all features of
The beauty you possess.
Perhaps you have been told
That I'm duplicitous,   50
Since you're distressed by this.
You'll know by outward signs
What I would say in words,
The next time you see me.

O freshly minted song,   55
Go sing this new refrain;
Rise early in the day
To greet the loveliest,
The best of all who love,
More blond than purest gold: 60
"Your love, which is so dear,
Vouchsafe the Notary,
A native of Lentini."

3 Canzone

Guiderdone aspetto avere
da voi, donna, cui servire
no m'enoia;
ancor che mi siate altera
sempre spero avere intera   5
d'amor gioia.
Non vivo in disperanza,
ancor che mi disfidi
la vostra disdegnanza,
ca spesse volte vidi, – ed è provato,   10
omo di poco affare
pervenire in gran loco:
se lo sape avanzare,
moltiplicar lo poco – ch'à 'quistato.

In disperanza no mi getto,   15
ch'io medesmo mi 'mprometto
d'aver bene,
di bon core la leanza
ch'i' vi porto, e la speranza
mi mantene.   20
Però no mi scoraggio
d'Amor che m'à distretto,
sì com'omo salvaggio
faraggio, com'è detto – ch'ello face:
per lo reo tempo ride,   25
sperando che poi pèra
lo laido aire che vede;
da donna troppo fera – spero pace.

S'io pur spero in allegranza,
fina donna, pïetanza   30
in voi si mova.
Fina donna, no mi siate
fera, poi tanta bieltate
in voi si trova,

3

I hope for recompense
From you, my lady, whom I'm not
Displeased to serve;
Although you treat me haughtily
I still hope to attain   5
Full joy of love.
I have not given up,
Although your arrogance
Makes me less confident:
For often I have seen, as is well known,   10
A man of modest means
Attain a lofty rank,
If he improves his worth
By multiplying what he has acquired.

I shall not give up hope,   15
For I myself intend
To have success;
My loyalty toward you
Is genuine, and hope
Will nurture me.   20
So I am not dismayed
By Love who's seized me fast,
For I intend to do
Precisely what they say a savage does:
When skies are grim he laughs,   25
Hoping that the gloom
He sees will fade away;
From one who's very cruel I hope for peace.

If I keep seeking joy through hope,
My perfect love, may mercy   30
Move your heart.
My perfect lady, don't be cruel,
Since so much loveliness
Is found in you:

ca donna ch'à bellezze   35
ed è senza pietade,
com'omo ch'à richezze
ed usa scarsitade – di ciò ch'àve;
se non è bene-apreso,
nodruto e insegnato,   40
da ogn'omo 'nd'è ripreso,
orruto e dispregiato – e posto a grave.

Donna mia, ch'eo non perisca,
s'eo vi prego, no vi 'ncresca
mia preghera.   45
Le bellezze che 'n voi pare
mi distringe, e lo sguardare
de la cera;
la figura piacente
lo core mi diranca: 50
quando voi tegno mente
lo spirito mi manca – e torna in ghiaccio:
né-mica mi spaventa
l'amoroso volere
di ciò che m'atalenta,   55
ch'eo no lo posso avere, – und'eo mi sfaccio.

For she who's beautiful   35
But lacks all sympathy
Is like a man of wealth
Who's parsimonious with what he has;
If he is not well-bred,
Refined and well-informed,   40
He'll be reproached by all,
Reviled, despised, and put in dire straits.

My fair, don't let me die,
I beg you, may my plea
Not anger you.   45
The beauty you display,
The look upon your face,
Leave me in pain.
That lovely mien of yours
Makes my heart break apart: 50
For when I look at you
My spirits lose their strength and turn to ice.
The fact I can't prevail
In no way will subdue
The yearning of my love   55
To gain what pleases it, so I'm destroyed.

4 Canzone

Amor non vole ch'io clami
merzede ch'onn'omo clama,
né che io m'avanti ch'ami,
ch'ogn'omo s'avanta ch'ama;
che lo servire ch'onn'omo   5
sape fare nonn-à nomo,
e no è in pregio di laudare
quello che sape ciascuno:
a voi, bella, tale dono
non vorria apresentare.   10

Per zo l'amore mi 'nsegna
ch'io non guardi a l'antra gente,
non vuol ch'io resembli a scigna
ch'ogni viso tene mente;
e per zo, madonna mia,   15
a voi non dimanderia
merzede né pïetanza,
che tanti son li amatori
ch'èste 'scita di savori
merzede per troppa usanza.   20

Ogni gioia ch'è più rara
tenut'è più prezïosa,
ancora che non sia cara
de l'altre più grazïosa;
ca s'èste orïentale   25
lo zafiro asai più vale,
ed à meno di vertute:
e per zo ne le merzede
lo mio core non v'accede,
perché l'uso l'à 'nvilute.   30

4

Love will not let me seek
The reward all men seek
Nor let me boast I love,
Since all men boast they love;
For service all can do   5
Will win no fame at all,
And there's but little praise
For what all men can do:
That gift on you, my fair,
I would not dare bestow.   10

And so I'm taught by love
To disregard the norm:
I mustn't mime an ape
That mimics what it sees;
And so, my dearest one,   15
I would not seek from you
Reward or sympathy,
Since lovers so abound
That, being overused,
All pity tastes quite bland.   20

The more a gem is rare
The more it's valuable,
Though it may not be deemed
As lovely as the rest;
For if it's from the east   25
The sapphire's worth much more,
Though it's less luminous.
My heart will brook from you
No gift of sympathy:
It's cheapened by wide use.   30

Inviluto li scolosmini
di quel tempo ricordato,
ch'erano sì gai e fini,
nulla gioi nonn-è trovato.
E·lle merzé siano strette,   35
nulla parte non sian dette
perché paian gioie nove:
nulla parte sian trovate
né dagli amador chiamate
infin che compie anni nove.   40

Senza merzede potete
saver, bella, 'l meo disio,
ch'assai meglio mi vedete
ch'io medesmo non mi veo;
e però s'a voi paresse   45
altro ch'esser non dovesse
per lo vostro amore avere,
unque gioia non ci perdiate,
cusì vol e te·'mistate,
inanzi voria morire.   50

All turquoise gems are cheap,
Although in former times
They were held chic and dear;
But now they lack appeal.
Let calls for pity be suppressed   35
And nowhere put in verse
So joy may be renewed.
No verse should offer space,
No lover ask for it,
At least for nine full years.   40

Though pity isn't sought,
You still know my desire,
For better you see me
Than I can see myself.
So if it seems to you   45
That all should stay the same
For me to win your love,
Don't waste your joy on that,
For so my love insists,
Or else I'd rather die.   50

5 Discordo

I   Dal core mi vene
    che gli occhi mi tene – rosata:
    spesso m'adivene
    che la cera ò bene – bagnata,
    quando mi sovene   5
    di mia bona spene – ch'ò data

    in voi, amorosa,
    benaventurosa.
    Però, se m'amate,
    già non vi 'ngannate – neiente,   10
    ca pur aspetando,
    in voi 'magginando,
    l'amor c'aggio in voi
    lo cor mi distrui, – avenente;
    ca·ss'io non temesse   15
    ch'a voi dispiacesse,
    ben m'aucideria,
    e non viverïâ – tormenti.

II Ca pur penare
    è disïare,   20
    giamai non fare
    mia diletanza:
    la rimembranza
    di voi, aulente cosa,
    gli ochi m'arosa   25
    d'un'aigua d'amore.

    Or potess'eo,
    o amore meo,
    come romeo
    venire ascoso,   30
    e disïoso
    con voi mi vedesse,
    non mi partisse
    dal vostro dolzore.

5

From my heart flows
A dew that fills my eyes;
I often find
My face completely bathed
When I recall   5
The worthy hope that I have placed

In you, my love,
The source of my good luck.
So if you love me too,
Do not at all misunderstand,   10
For since I'm forced to wait
And dream of you,
The love I bear for you,
My fair, destroys my heart;
So if I did not fear   15
That you would be upset,
I'd surely take my life,
And cease to live in pain.

For to desire
Means constant suffering,   20
To never have
My pleasure satisfied:
Remembering you,
Sweet-scented one,
Engulfs my eyes   25
With tears of love.

If I could now,
My dearest love,
Come secretly disguised
In pilgrim dress,   30
Full of desire,
And find myself with you,
I'd never part
From your sweet company.

III   Dal vostro lato   35
      [...] allungato,
      be·ll'ò provato
      mal che non salda:
      Tristano Isalda
      non amau sì forte;   40
      ben mi par morte
      non vedervi fiore.

      Vostro valore
      ch'adorna ed invia
      donne e donzelle,   45
      l'avisaturi
      di voi, donna mia,
      son gli ochi belli:
      pens'a tutore
      quando vi vedia   50
      con gioi novelli.

IV   «Hoi tu, meo core,
      perché non ti more?
      Rispondi, che fai?
      Perché [...] doli – così?»   55
      «Non ti rispondo,
      ma ben ti confondo
      se tosto non vai
      là ove voli – con mi:
      la fresca cera   60
      tempesta e dispera;
      in pensiero m'ài
      miso e 'n cordoglio – per ti».

V   Così, bella, – si favella
      lo mi' cor conmeco: 65
      di persona – no·m ragiona,
      né parlo né dico:
      sì curale – e naturale
      di voi amor mi piace,
      ch'ogni vista – mi par trista   70
      ch'altra donna face:

By being far   35
… apart from you
I've borne a wound
That never heals:
Sir Tristan did not love
Isolde with such zeal;   40
It surely seems like death
To see you not at all.

Your worthiness
Which gilds and shows the way
To ladies and young girls,   45
The messengers,
My lady, of your worth,
Are your own lovely eyes:
I always think about
The time I saw you last   50
With newfound joy.

"Alas, my heart,
Why not just die?
What are you doing? Speak!
Why grieve like this?"   55
"I won't reply,
But I shall ruin you
If you don't come with me
At once where I desire:
Her lovely face   60
Is angry and forlorn;
You've put me in distress
And grief on your behalf."

In just this way, my love,
My heart shares words with me: 65
It speaks of no one else,
And I as well will not.
I like the heartfelt, inborn love
I have for you so much
That every other lady's face   70
Seems sorry by compare:

ca·ss'io veglio – o sonno piglio,
lo mio cor no 'nsonna,
senno schietto – sì m'à stretto
pur di voi, madonna.   75

VI Sì m'è dura – e scura – figura
di quantonqu'eo veo,
gli occhi avere – e vedere – e volere
altro non disio;
trecce sciolte – ni avolte – ni adolte,   80
né bruna né bianca
[...] – [...] – [...]
[...] -anca].
Gioia complita – norita, – mi 'nvita:
voi siete più fina,   85
che s'io faccio – sollaccio – ch'io piaccio,
vostro amor mi mina

dotrina, – e benvolenza.
La vostra benvolenza
mi dona canoscenza   90
di servire a chiasenza
quella che più m'agenza,
e aggio ritemenza
per troppa sovenenza.

VII E no·m porta – Amor che sporta   95
e tira a ogne freno,
e non corre, – sì che scorre,
peramore fino.
Ben vorria, – e non lasseria
per nulla leanza,   100
s'io sapesse – ch'io morisse,
sì mi stringe amanza.
Tutto credo, – e non discredo,
che la mia venuta
dea placere – ed alegrire   105
de la [...] veduta.

For though I stir or sleep,
My heart remains awake,
So fast it has me bound
To you alone, my fair.   75

The sight of everything I see
Is cruel and unbearable,
I have no eyes or wish to see
Or long for someone else;
Nor tresses flowing, bound or preened,   80
brunette or blonde
...

...
A perfect, cultured joy appeals to me:
You are the most refined,   85
Since if I show delight that pleases you,
Your love and your goodwill

Bring wisdom to me.
And your goodwill
Enables me to know   90
The way to serve at will
The one I like the most,
Though countless memories
Have wakened fear in me.

I'm not enthralled by love   95
That's rash and lacks restraint,
Mine does not rush, but flows
And is refined.
I'd want this love, and would not be
Disloyal, ever, even if   100
I knew that I would die,
So tightly love embraces me.
I truly think, and do not doubt,
My coming will bring joy,
And make you glad   105
To ... see me.

VIII Ma sempre-mai non sento
      vostro comandamento,
      non ò confortamento
      del vostro avenimento,   110
      ch'io ristò e non canto
      sì ch'a voi piaccia tanto,
      e mandovi infratanto
      saluti e dolze pianto;
      e piango per usaggio,   115
      giamai non rideraggio
      mentre non vederaggio
      lo vostro bel visaggio.
      Ragione aggio,
      ed altro non faraggio,   120
      né poraggio,
      tal è lo mi' coraggio,

  IX ch'altre parole
      no vole,
      ma dole   125
      de li parlamenti
      de la genti:
      non consenti
      che parli né che dolenti,
      e aggio veduta   130
      perlasciare
      la tenuta
      de lo meo dolce penzare.

   X Sì como – noi
      che somo – d'un cor dui,   135
      ed ora – plui
      ched ancora – non fui,
      di voi, – bel viso,
      sono priso
      e conquiso;   140

But I have not as yet
Heard your command,
Nor can I rest assured
That you will come;   110
And so I cease to sing
Until you change your mind,
And meanwhile send along
My greetings and sweet sighs;
I'm used to shedding tears,   115
And I won't smile again
Until I gaze upon
The beauty of your face.
I'm in the right,
And won't and can't   120
Do otherwise,
Such is my will,

For further words
She won't abide,
Yet she endures   125
The gossiping
That others make:
She won't consent
To let me speak or grieve,
And I can see   130
Abandoning
The custody
Of my sweet thoughts.

Since we are two
Who have one heart,   135
And now more so
Than ever was before,
I'm seized
And overcome
By your sweet face;   140

che fra dormentare
mi fa levare
e intrare
in sì gran foco
ca per poco   145
non m'aucido
de lo strido
ch'io ne gitto,
[…] -etto]
[…] -ete]   150
ch'io non vegna là ove siete,
rimembrando,
bella, quando
con voi mi vedea
sollazzando   155
ed istando
in gioi, sì com' far solea.

XI   Per quant'aggio di gioia
tant'aggio mala noia:
la mia vita è croia   160
sanza voi vedendo.
Cantando […] aivo
or vivo pur pensivo
e tutta gente ischivo,
sì ch'io vo fuggendo,   165
pur cherendo – ond'io m'asconda:
onde lo core m'abonda
e per gli occhi fuori gronda,
sì dolcemente fonda\
com' lo fino oro che fonda.   170

Orma' risponda, – mandatemi a dire:
«Voi che martiri – per me sofferite?»;
«Ben vi dovrete – infra lo cor dolire
de' mie' martire, – se vi sovenite
come sete – lontana,   175
sovrana – de lo core prossimana».

For in my sleep
I am aroused
And enter
Flames so great
I nearly   145
Slay myself
With shrieks
That I cast forth,
...
...   150
That I can't reach your side,
Remembering,
My fair, the times
I found myself
With you at play   155
And being content,
As used to be my wont.

For all the joy I have
I've just as much unhappiness:
My life is vile   160
Not seeing you.
When singing ... I'm alive
But now I am upset
And turn from everyone,
So that I must abscond   165
And seek somewhere to hide;
Hence my heart overflows
And floods my eyes with tears
That flow as sweetly as
The purest liquid gold.   170

Now answer me, command that I be asked:
"What pain do you endure for me?"
"Indeed your heart should feel the pain
Of my distress, if you recall
How far away you are,   175
Exalted one so near my heart."

6   Canzone

La 'namoranza – disïosa
che dentro a lo mi' cor è nata
di voi, madonna, è pur chiamata
merzé se fusse aventurosa;
e poi ch'i' non trovo pietanza,   5
per paura o per dottare
s'io perdo amare,
Amor comanda ch'io faccia arditanza.

Grande arditanza – e coraggiosa
in guiderdone Amor m'à data,   10
e vuol che donna sia 'quistata
per forza di gioia amorosa:
ma' troppo è villana credanza
che donna deggia incominzare,
ma vergognare   15
perch'io cominzi non è mispregianza.

Di mispregianza – Amor mi scusa
se gioia per me è cominzata
di voi che tant'ò disïata,
e sonne in vita cordogliosa: 20
ca, bella, sanza dubitanza,
tutte fïate in voi mirare,
veder mi pare
una maraviliosa simiglianza.

Tanto siete maravigliosa   25
quand'i' v'ò bene affigurata
ch'altro parete che 'ncarnata,
se non ch'io spero in voi, gioiosa,
ma tanto tarda la speranza
solamente per donare   30
oi malparlare
Amor non vuol ch'io perda mia intendanza.

6

The passionate desire
Conceived within my heart,
My fair, calls ceaselessly
On you so mercy might bear fruit;
But since I find no sympathy,   5
Lest I should lose my love
Through fear and dread,
Love charges me to take more risk.

More risk and derring-do
Love grants me as a gift,   10
And wants my lady to be won
By dint of joyous love.
It's very foolish to believe
That ladies must initiate,
But my fear to begin   15
Should not be viewed as disrespect.

Love pardons me of disrespect
From when my joy began with you
Whom I have craved so much
That I live life in agony.   20
Because, my fair, without a doubt,
Each time I look at you
I seem to see
An image that is wonderful.

You look so wonderful   25
When I've imagined you
That you seem more than flesh and blood,
For I still place my hope in you,
But though hope's slow to come
Love won't let me lose my desire   30
For just some gossiping
Or slandering.

Molt'è gran cosa ed inoiosa
chi vede ciò che più li agrata,
e via d'un passo è più dotata   35
che d'oltremare in Saragosa,
e di bataglia, ov'om si lanza
a spad'e lanza, in terra o mare,
e non pensare
di bandire una donna per dottanza.   40

Nulla bandita m'è dottosa
se non di voi, donna pregiata,
ch'anti vorria morir di spata
ch'i' voi vedesse currucciosa;
ma tanto avete caunoscianza,   45
ben mi dovreste perdonare
e comportare,
s'io perdo gioia che·sso m'aucide amanza.

It's difficult and maddening
For one to see what brings most joy
And fear the way that leads to it   35
More than the path across the sea
To Syracuse, or skirmishing
With lance and sword, on land or sea,
And not think to
Declare love for one's lady out of fear.   40

I do not fear to make known any name
Except, my worthy, yours,
For I would sooner die by sword
Than see you be displeased;
But knowing this so well,   45
You really should consent
To pardon me,
For love will slay me if I lose my joy.

7   Canzone

Ben m'è venuto prima cordoglienza,
poi benvoglienza – orgoglio m'è rendente
di voi, madonna, contra mia soffrenza:
non è valenza – far male a sofrente.
Tant'è potente vostra signoria,   5
ch'avendo male più v'amo ogni dia:
però tuttor la troppo sicuranza
ubrïa caunoscenza e onoranza.

Adunque, amor, ben fora convenenza
d'aver temenza – como l'altra gente,   10
che tornano la lor discaunoscenza
a la credenza – de lo benvogliente:
chi è temente fugge villania,
e per coverta tal fa cortesia,
ch'eo non vorria da voi, donna, semblanza,   15
se da lo cor non vi venisse amanza.

E chi a torto batte o fa increscenza,
di far plagenza – penza, poi si pente:
però mi pasco di bona credenza,
ch'Amor comenza – prim'a dar tormente;   20
dunque più gente seria la gioi mia,
se per soffrir l'orgoglio s'umilìa
e la ferezza torna in pïetanza;
be·llo pò fare Amor, ch'ell'è su' usanza.

Eo non vi faccio, donna, contendenza,   25
ma ubidenza, – e amo coralmente;
però non deggio planger penitenza,
ca nullo senza – colpa è penitente.
Naturalmente – avene tuttavia
ch'omo s'orgoglia a chi lo contrarìa;   30
ma vostr'orgoglio passa sorcoitanza,
che dismisura contra umilïanza.

7

A sense of anguish has come over me,
Because my love for you spawns your disdain,
Since I, my lady, suffer patiently:
No honor's won in harming sufferers.
So potent is your dominance   5
That, even hurt, I love you more each day:
Hence always will excessive confidence
Make one forget what's wise and honorable.

And so, my love, it would be opportune
If you were prudent, just as others are   10
Who modify their foolish ways
To bring more credit to their love.
One who is wise avoids discourtesy,
But courtesy that's hypocritical
I would not like to see in you, my fair,   15
Unless your love came from your heart.

But one who strikes unjustly or offends
Thinks others like his acts, and then repents:
I stay alive through steadfast confidence,
Since Love begins by causing pain at first.   20
So my felicity would be supreme
If for my patience you allay your pride
And turn your cruelty to sympathy;
Love does this well, because it's his routine.

I will not, lady, disagree with you,   25
But shall obey and love you utterly;
So I am not obliged to be contrite,
Since one who hasn't sinned need not repent.
It's always natural for one to make
A show of pride before an enemy;   30
But what pride you show outdoes arrogance,
Exceeding measure, unlike humbleness.

E voi che sete senza percepenza,
como Florenza – che d'orgoglio sente,
guardate a Pisa di gran canoscenza,   35
che teme tenza – d'orgogliosa gente:
sì lungiamente – orgoglio m'à in bailia,
Melano del carroccio par che sia;
e si si tarda l'umile speranza,
chi sofr'acompl'e vince ogni tardanza.   40

And you who lack a penetrating eye,
Like Florence, which behaves with arrogance,
Direct your eyes on Pisa, ever wise,   35
Which fears a feud with people who are proud:
For quite some time your pride has mastered me,
You're like Milan with its war chariot;
But while my humble hope's been put in check,
The patient win and conquer all delay.   40

8   Canzone

Donna, eo languisco e no so qua·speranza
mi dà fidanza – ch'io non mi disfidi;
e se merzé e pietanza in voi non trovo,
perduta provo – lo chiamar merzede;
che tanto lungiamente ò custumato,   5
palese ed in celato,
pur di merzé cherere,
ch'i' non·ssaccio altro dire;
e s'altri m'adomanda ched aggio eo,
eo non so dir se non «Merzé, per Deo!».   10

Amore non fue giusto partitore,
ch'io pur v'adore – e voi non mi 'ntendate:
sì com'eo presi a voi merzé chiamare,
ben dovea dare – a voi cor di pietate,
ca tutesor cad eo merzé chiamasse,   15
in voi, donna, trovasse
gran core d'umiltate;
se non tutte fïate
facestemi a lo meno esta 'mistanza,
mille merzé valesse una pietanza.   20

Donna, gran maraviglia mi donate,
che 'n voi sembrate – sono tanto alore:
passate di bellezze ogn'altra cosa,
come la rosa – passa ogn'altro fiore,
e l'adornezze quali v'acompagna   25
lo cor mi lancia e sagna:
per mi sta asai plui
merzé che nonn-è in voi,
e se merzé con voi, bella, statesse,
null'altra valenza più mi valesse.   30

8

My Love, I suffer and don't know how hope
Can make me confident I won't lose faith;
And if I find you lack all sympathy
I'll feel that seeking mercy has no point;
It's been my habit for so long,   5
Both secretly and openly,
To always sue for sympathy,
So I am at a loss for words;
And if I'm asked what troubles me,
I can but plead "Have mercy, Lord!"   10

Love has dispensed with an unequal hand,
For I adore you while you love me not:
When I began to seek your sympathy,
He should have filled your heart with pity's balm,
Then every time I asked for sympathy   15
I'd find in you, my love,
A very humble heart;
And if not all the time,
Bestow on me at least this show of love,
A thousand pleas deserve one act of pity.   20

My Lady, how you do astonish me,
So many fragrances seem wed in you:
You best in beauty everything,
Just as a rose bests every flower,
And beauty that accompanies you   25
Impales my heart and makes it bleed:
But it means more to me
That pity can't be found in you,
And yet if pity found a home in you,
No other worth would be worth more.   30

Non mi ricredo di merzé chiamare,
ca contare – audivi a molta gente
che lo lëone èste di tale usato
che quand'è airato – più fellonamente,
per cosa ch'omo face si ricrede   35
'· segno di merzede:
per merzé gira in pace.
Gentile ira mi piace,
ond'io per mercé faccio ogne mi' fatto,
ca per mercé s'apaga un gran misfatto.   40

Sì com' quelli che·ffanno a·llor nemici,
ch'ogn'om mi dici: – «merzede ò trovato»,
ed io che·ffaccio, così ratto provo
e non trovo – merzede in cui son dato.
Madonna, in voi nonn-aquistai gran preio   45
se non pure lo peio,
e per ciò si ch'om batte
[...] in altrui fatte,
e s'egli 'n altro vince, in questo perde,
e 'n voi chi più ci pensa più ci sperde.   50

I won't relent from seeking sympathy,
For I have often heard it said
A lion is by instinct so disposed
That when it is most savagely enraged
It will relent if one appeals   35
For sympathy:
For pity it departs in peace.
This noble wrath I like,
So all I do will be for sympathy,
For pity can redeem a great offense.   40

As others do before their enemies,
Of whom all tell me "Pity have I found,"
I do as well myself, and quickly seek
Yet find no pity in my chosen one.
My love, from you I've gotten no reward   45
Except the worst each time,
And so one fights this way
… in another's deeds,
But if one wins elsewhere, one loses here:
Who thinks about you most has most to lose.   50

9   Canzone

Troppo son dimorato
i·llontano paese:
non so in che guisa possa soferire
che son cotanto stato
senza in cui si mise   5
tutte bellezze d'amore e servire.
Molto tardi mi pento,
e dico che follia
me n'à fatto alungare;
lasso, ben veggio e sento,   10
mort'e' fusse, dovria
a madonna tornare.

Ca s'io sono alungato,
a null'om non afesi
quant'a me solo, ed i' ne so' al perire;   15
io ne so' il danneggiato
poi madonna misfesi,
mio è 'l dannaggio ed ogne languire;
ca lo suo avenimento
d'amar mi travaglìa,   20
e comandami a dare,
a quella a cui consento,
core e corpo in baglìa,
e nulla non mi pare.

Dunqua son io sturduto?   25
Ciò saccio certamente,
con' quelli ch'à cercato ciò che tene,
così m'è adivenuto,
che, lasso, l'avenente
eo vo cercando, ed ò noie e pene.   30

9

Too long have I resided
In a far-off place:
I don't know how I shall abide
My lengthy stay away
From her in whom I've placed   5
The pleasure and the service of my love.
Quite late I now repent,
And know that foolishness
Made me go far away;
Unhappy, I now see   10
And know, were I to die,
I still should go back to my love.

For if I've gone away,
I've done no harm to anyone
As much as to myself, who's close to death;   15
It's I who have been harmed
For having shown my lady disrespect,
Mine are the pain and all the suffering;
Indeed her beauty still
Torments me through my love,   20
And forces me to give,
To her to whom I yield,
My heart and being to rule,
And this to me seems nothing.

Then why am I so stunned?   25
I know quite certainly,
Like one who's sought what he already has,
For so it's been with me,
That I, though sad, keep searching
For my love, and find but grief and pain.   30

Cotanto n'ò dolore
e vengiamento e doglia,
vedere non potere
cotanto di dolzore
amore e bona voglia,   35
ch'io l'ò creduto avere.

Deo, com'aggio falluto,
che cusì lungiamente
non son tornato a la mia donn' a spene!
Lasso, chi m'à tenuto?   40
Follia dilivramente,
che m'à levato da gioia e di bene.
Ochi e talento e core
ciascun per sé s'argoglia,
disïando vedere   45
madonna mia a tuttore,
quella che non s'argoglia
inver' lei lo mio volere.

Non vo' più soferenza,
né dimorare oimai   50
senza madonna, di cui moro stando;
ch'Amor mi move 'ntenza
e dicemi: «che·ffai?
la tua donna si muor di te aspettando».
Questo detto mi lanza,   55
e fammi trangosciare
sì lo core, moraggio
se più faccio tardanza:
tosto farò reo stare
di lei e di me dannaggio.   60

So heavy is my woe,
My spite and bitterness,
I lack the power to see
So great a fund of charm,
Such love and such good will,   35
Which I had thought I had.

Oh God, how wrong I've been,
Because it's been so long
I've not returned to her with hope.
Alas, who's held me back?   40
My foolish love, of course,
Which has divested me of joy and love.
My eyes, desire, and heart
Each by itself is stirred,
Desiring to regard   45
My lady constantly,
The one who isn't stirred
By my desire for her.

I'm done with standing pat,
And living far away   50
Without my love, for whom I die.
For Love contends with me,
And asks: "What are you doing?
Your lady dies awaiting you."
These words cut to the quick   55
And so afflict my heart
That I shall not survive
If I delay much more:
I'll quickly end the harm
That's done to her and me.   60

10

Non so se 'n gioia mi sia
d'amor la mia intendanza
'nver la [...]

10 (Fragment)

I don't know if my love
For her will bring me joy
...

11   Canzone

Uno disïo d'amore sovente
mi ten la mente,
temer mi face e miso m'à in erranza:
non saccio s'io lo taccia o dica nente
di voi, più gente,   5
no vi dispiaccia, tant'ò dubitanza.
Ca s'eo lo taccio vivo in penetenza,
ch'Amor mi 'ntenza
di ciò che pò avenire:
e' poria romanere   10
in danno che poria sortire a manti,
se·llor è detto: «guardisi davanti».

E s'eo l'ò detto, temo molto piue
non spiaccia a voi,
a cui servir mi sforzo, donna fina,   15
ca semo, per leanza ch'è 'ntra noi,
d'uno cor dui:
temer mi face Amor che mi mena.
E se la mia temenza penserete,
più m'amerete,   20
perché le mie paure
non son se non d'amore:
chi ciò non teme, male amar poria,
e tutta mia paura è gelosia.

Geloso sono d'amor m'adovene,   25
così mi stene,
ch'Amore è piena cosa di paura:
e chi bene ama una cosa che tene,
vive 'nde in pene,
che teme no la perda per ventura.   30
Donqu'è ragion ch'eo trovi pïetanza
e perdonanza,
ca s'eo in voi troppo isparlo
non sono eo che parlo:
Amore è che tacente fa tornare   35
lo ben parlante, e lo muto parlare.

11

Frequently an amorous desire
Pervades my thoughts,
Arouses fear in me and fosters doubt:
I do not know if I should speak of you
Or not, most noble one,   5
So greatly do I fear displeasing you.
For if I'm silent I will live in want,
Since Love warns me
About what might ensue:
I could remain impaired,   10
Which might affect far more than just a few,
If they are told: "Now watch your step."

And if I spoke, more greatly would I fear
Displeasing you,
Most gracious lady, whom I strive to serve,   15
For we, who share a fealty, are two
With just one heart:
My leader, Love, arouses fear in me.
And if you think about the fear I have,
You'll love me more,   20
Since all my fears
Are wrought by love alone:
One lacking fear might love improperly,
And all my fears are born of jealousy.

It happens I'm made jealous by my love,   25
So bound am I,
For Love is something that is full of fear:
And if one loves intensely what one has,
One lives in pain,
For fear of losing it through some mischance.   30
This justifies my seeking pity
And forgiveness too,
For if I speak too much of you
It is not I who speak:
It's Love who silences the eloquent,   35
And he as well who makes the silent speak.

Donqua s'Amore non vole ch'eo taccia,
non vi dispiaccia
s'Amore è d'uno folle pensamento:
quell'è la gioia che più mi solazza,   40
par che mi sfazza,
ch'eo ebbi di voi, donna, compimento;
ma no·l vorria avere avuto intando
che vo pensando
e convenmi partire,   45
in altra parte gire:
la gioi che di voi, donna, aggio avuta,
no la mi credo aver mai sì compiuta.

Per ciò vorria ch'eo l'avesse ad avere,
ed a vedere,   50
che di ciò nasce che mi discoraia:
non adovegna con' al mio temere
(vergogna è a dire),
che sicuranza ormai nulla no 'nd'aia.
Ma sì io son folle ne lo mio pensare   55
per troppo amare,
ca spero in voi, avenente,
ch'eo non serò perdente:
sì come da voi ebbi guiderdone,
mi traggerete fuor d'ogne casone.   60

So if Love will not have me hold my tongue,
Take no offense
That Love is just a madcap thought.
The joy that pleases me the most of all,   40
Which seems to ruin me,
Is consummation you gave me, my fair.
I wish, however, I'd not had it yet
When I reflect
How I must leave   45
And go elsewhere:
The joy that I once had from you, my love,
I think I'll never have so perfect once again.

That's why I wish I had it still to have
And to anticipate,   50
Since it's the source of my unhappiness:
May it not come about just as I fear
(I am ashamed to say)
That I should lack assurance of your love.
But so completely am I mad in thought   55
From too much love
That, lovely one, I hope
I'll never lose your love:
Just as I once received your recompense,
You'll rescue me from every quandary.   60

12   Canzone

Amando lungiamente,
disïo ch'io vedesse
quell'ora ch'io piacesse
com'io valesse – a voi, donna valente.
Meravigliosamente   5
mi sforzo s'io potesse
ch'io cotanto valesse,
ch'a voi paresse – lo mio affar piacente.
Vorria servire a piacimento
là 'v'è tutto piacere,   10
e convertire – lo meo parlamento
a ciò ch'eo sento:
per intendanza de le mie parole
veggiate come lo meo cor si dole.

Non dole ch'aggia doglia,   15
madonna, in voi amare,
anti mi fa allegrare
in voi pensare – l'amorosa voglia:
con gioi par che m'acoglia
lo vostro innamorare,   20
e per dolce aspettare
veder mi pare – ciò che mi s'orgoglia.
Ma d'una cosa mi cordoglio,
ch'eo non so in veritate
che voi sacciate – lo ben ch'eo vi voglio: 25
a ciò mi doglio,
non posso dir di cento parti l'una
l'amor ch'eo porto a la vostra persona.

Se l'amor ch'eo vi porto
non posso dire in tutto,   30
vagliami alcun bon motto,
che per un frutto – piace tutto un orto,

12

In loving for so long,
I wish that I could see
The time when you'd be pleased
By what I'm worth to you, my worthy one.
Extraordinarily   5
I strive so that I might
Acquire the worthiness
To make my love seem valuable to you.
I'd like to serve befittingly
Where all my pleasure dwells,   10
And make my choice of words conform
To what I feel:
By understanding what I say
You'll see how my heart's overcome with pain.

The pain I feel in loving you,   15
My lady, does not hurt
But makes me glad to think
That you might harbor love as well.
With joyfulness your love
Appears to welcome me,   20
Yet thanks to my sweet wait
I seem to see what treats me with disdain.
But I am saddened by one fact,
That I don't truly know
If you perceive the love I have for you: 25
What makes me ache
Is that I cannot tell a hundredth part
Of all the love I bear for you.

If I cannot express in full
The love I bear for you,   30
This adage makes my point,
That one piece validates a garden's fruit;

e per un bon conforto
si lassa un gran corrotto
e ritorna in disdutto: 35
a ciò non dotto, – tal speranza porto.
E se alcun torto mi vedete,
ponete mente a voi,
che bella piui – per orgoglio siete,
che ben sapete   40
ch'orgoglio non è gioia, m'a voi convene
e tutto quanto veggio a voi sta bène.

E tutto quanto veggio
mi pare avenantezze
e somma di bellezze;   45
altre ricchezze – né gio' non disio
e nulla donna veo
ch'aggia tante adornezze
che '·le vostre altezze
non bassezze, – là unde innamorìo.   50
E se [...], madonna mia,
amasse io voi e voi meve,
se fosse neve – foco mi parria,
e notte e dia
e tuttavia – mentre ch'avraggio amore,   55
e chi ben ama ritorna in dolore.

Non so com'eo vi paro
né che di me farete;
ancider mi potrete
e no mi trovarete – core varo,   60
ma tuttavia d'un airo,
cotanto mi piacete;
e morto mi vedete
se no m'avrete – a lo vostro riparo:
a lo conforto di pietanza   65
che incozzi a lo core,
e li occhi fore – piangano d'amanza
e d'allegranza,
con abondanza – de lo dolce pianto
lo bel visaggio bagni tutto quanto.   70

And through kind comforting
A heavy grief is left behind
And is turned into joy: 35
Of this I have no fear, my hope's so strong.
And if you find some fault in me,
Look at yourself instead,
For being proud makes you most beautiful,
Though you know well   40
That pride's not bliss, but it is suitable
And all I see befits you perfectly.

And everything I see
Seems beautiful to me
And beauty unsurpassed;   45
I crave no other luxury or joy
And see no lady quite
So full of loveliness
Whose worth is anything but base
Compared with yours, which spawned my love.   50
And if ..., my lady,
I were to love you and you me,
If this were snow, then it would seem like fire,
As night would day,
And ever for as long as I'm in love,   55
Though one who truly loves revisits pain.

I don't know how I seem to you
Nor what you'll do concerning me.
Though slay me if you will,
You'll find my heart unwavering   60
And always of one mind,
So much do I love you;
But you will find me dead
If you won't have me in your custody:
I wish you'd strike my heart   65
To comfort me with sympathy
And make my eyes weep many tears of love
And happiness,
So that I fully bathe your lovely face
With an abundance of my tender tears.   70

13 Canzonetta

Madonna mia, a voi mando
in gioi li mei sospiri,
ca lungiamente amando
non vi porea mai dire
com'era vostro amante   5
e lealmente amava,
e però ch'eo dottava
non vo facea sembrante.

Tanto set'alta e grande
ch'eo v'amo pur dottando,   10
e non so cui vo mande
per messaggio parlando,
und'eo prego l'Amore,
a cui prega ogni amanti,
li mei sospiri e pianti   15
vo pungano lo core.

Ben vorria, s'eo potesse,
quanti sospiri eo getto,
ch'ogni sospiro avesse
spirito e intelletto,   20
ch'a voi, donna, d'amare
dimandasser pietanza,
da poi ch'e' per dottanza
non vo posso parlare.

Voi, donna, m'aucidete   25
e allegiate a penare:
da poi che voi vedete
ch'io vo dotto parlare,
perché non mi mandate
tuttavia confortando,   30
ch'eo non desperi amando
de la vostra amistate?

13

My lady, I send you
My sighs abrim with joy,
Since loving for so long
I could not ever say
That you were my beloved   5
And that my love was loyal,
And that I kept it hid
Because I felt afraid.

You are so noble and so great
I love you yet have fear;   10
I don't know whom to send
As messenger to speak to you,
So I appeal to Love,
To whom all lovers plead,
To let my sighs and cries   15
Pierce deep into your heart.

If I were able, I should like,
For all the sighs I heave,
That every sigh could be
Alive and have a voice,   20
To seek from you, my dear,
Compassion for my love of you,
Because the fear I have
Won't let me speak to you.

My lady, you destroy my life   25
Yet mitigate my pain:
Since you can see quite well
That I'm afraid to speak to you,
Why don't you send to me
Your comfort constantly,   30
Lest I despair, for love,
Of my friendship with you?

Vostra cera plagente,
mercé quando vo chiamo,
mi 'ncalcia fortemente   35
ch'io v'ami più ch'io v'amo,
ch'io non vi poteria
più coralmente amare,
ancor che più penare
poria, sì, donna mia.   40

In gran dilettanz'era,
madonna, in quello giorno
quando ti formai in cera
le bellezze d'intorno:
più bella mi parete   45
ca Isolda la bronda,
amorosa gioconda
che sovr'ogn'altra sete.

Ben sai ch'e' son vostr'omo,
s'a voi non dispiacesse,   50
ancora che 'l meo nomo,
madonna, non dicesse:
per vostro amor fui nato,
nato fui da Lentino;
dunqua debb'esser fino,   55
da poi ch'a voi son dato.

That pleasing face of yours,
When I seek sympathy,
Incites me forcefully   35
To love you more than now,
But I could not love you
More strongly with my heart,
Though I could suffer more,
In truth, my lady fair.   40

I felt such great delight,
My lady, on the day
When I portrayed your face
With all the beauty you possess:
You seem more beautiful   45
Than fair Isolde was,
My sweetheart full of joy,
For you best each and all.

You know quite well I'm yours,
I hope you're not displeased,   50
Although my name, my fair,
I've never said to you:
For your love I was born,
And in Lentino I was born;
So my love must be true,   55
Since I am meant for you.

14 Canzone

S'io doglio no è meraviglia
e s'io sospiro e lamento:
amor lontano mi piglia
dogliosa pena ch'eo sento,
membrando ch'eo sia diviso   5
di vedere lo bel viso
per cui peno e sto 'n tormento.

Allegranza lo vedere
mi donava proximano,
lo contrario deggio avere   10
ch'eo ne son fatto lontano:
s'eo veggendo avea allegranza,
or no la veggio ò pesanza
mi distringe e tene mano.

Lo meo core eo l'aio lassato   15
a la dolze donna mia:
dogliomi ch'eo so' allungiato
da sì dolze compagnia;
co·madonna sta lo core,
che de lo meo petto è fore,   20
e dimora in sua bailia.

Dogliomi e adiro sovente
de lo core che dimora
con madonna mia avenente,
in sì gran bona-ventura: 25
odio e invidio tale affare,
che con lei non posso stare
né veder la sua figura.

14

It's no surprise I grieve
And sigh and make lament:
A distant love inflicts
A grievous pain to bear,
Reminding me how I'm deprived   5
Of seeing her sweet face
Which makes me smart with pain.

To see her close nearby
Brought happiness to me;
Now I must bear the opposite,   10
For I am far from her.
If I was happy seeing her,
Now that I can't brings pain,
Which grips me and holds sway.

I gave my heart away   15
To my sweet lady love:
I grieve that I'm apart
From such sweet company;
My lady has my heart,
Which lives outside my breast,   20
And dwells beneath her rule.

I grieve and often feel distraught
Because my heart resides
With her, my lovely one,
In such a happy state: 25
I hate and loathe this plight,
For I can't dwell with her
Or see her lovely form.

Sovente mi doglio e adiro,
fuggir mi fanno allegrezze;   30
tuttavia raguardo e miro
le suoe adornate fattezze,
lo bel viso e l'ornamento
e lo dolze parlamento,
occhi, ahi, vaghi e bronde trezze.   35

I often grieve and feel distraught,
All pleasure flees from me;   30
I keep on gazing at
The grace of her fine looks,
Her lovely face and charm,
The sweetness of her speech,
Her lovely eyes, ah, and blond hair.   35

15

Amore, paura m'incalcia
in manti lochi aventurosi

15   (Fragment)

O Love, fear spurs me to embark
On many bold and daring quests

16   Canzone

Poi no mi val merzé né ben servire
inver' mia donna, in cui tegno speranza
e amo lealmente,
non so che cosa mi possa valere:
se di me no le prende pïetanza,   5
ben morrò certamente.
Per nente – mi cangiao lo suo talento,
und'eo tormento – e vivo in gran dottanza,
e son di molte pene sofferente.

Sofferente – seraggio al so piacere,   10
di bon core e di pura leanza
la servo umilemente:
anzi vorrea per ella pena avere
che per null'altra bene con baldanza,
tanto le so' ubidente.   15
Ardente – son di far suo piacimento,
e mai no alento – d'aver sua membranza,
in quella in cui disïo spessamente.

Spessamente disïo e sto al morire,
membrando che m'à miso in ubrïanza   20
l'amorosa piacente;
senza misfatto no·m dovea punire,
di far partenza de la nostra amanza,
poi tant'è caunoscente.
Temente – so' e non ò confortamento,   25
poi valimento – no·m dà, ma pesanza,
e fallami di tutto 'l suo conventi.

16

Since neither mercy nor performing deeds
On her behalf avails, though she's my hope,
The one I truly love,
I do not know what would avail:
If she won't grant me pity soon,   5
Then surely I will die.
For naught she changed her attitude toward me,
And so I feel great pain and live in fear,
And shoulder many forms of agony.

My suffering will be for her delight,   10
Sincerely and with faultless loyalty
I serve her humbly:
I'd rather suffer pain because of her
Than happily engage some other love,
So faithfully I serve.   15
I burn to do whatever pleases her
And never shall I cease to think about
The one whom I desire incessantly.

I yearn incessantly and lie near death,
Recalling that my beautiful beloved   20
Has quite forgotten me;
Without some fault she shouldn't have punished me,
By bringing to an end the love we share,
Since she is very wise.
I'm in a state of fear and unconsoled   25
Because she brings me misery, not help,
And fails to keep the pledge she made to me.

Conventi – mi fece di ritenere
e donaomi una gio' per rimembranza,
ch'eo stesse allegramente.   30
Or la m'à tolta per troppo savere,
dice che 'n altra parte ò mia 'ntendanza,
ciò so veracemente:
non sente – lo meo cor tal fallimento,
né ò talento – di far misleanza,   35
ch'eo la cangi per altra al meo vivente.

Vivente – donna non creo che partire
potesse lo mio cor di sua possanza,
non fosse sì avenente,
per ch'io lasciar volesse d'ubidire   40
quella che pregio e bellezze inavanza
e fami star sovente
la mente – d'amoroso pensamento:
non aggio abento, – tanto 'l cor mi lanza
co li riguardi degli occhi ridente.   45

She made a pledge to keep me as her love
And to remember her gave me her joy,
So I would be content.   30
Now she has taken it away from me,
Presuming that I have another love,
And says I know that's true:
My heart is unaware of such a sin,
And I've no wish to be disloyal and trade   35
My love for someone else as long as I live.

No living lady has the power, I think,
To separate my heart from her command,
However beautiful,
Such that I'd wish to cease obeying her   40
Whom loveliness and excellence exalt
And who so often fills
My mind with many thoughts concerning love:
I find no peace, so often does she pierce
My heart with glances from her smiling eyes.   45

17   Canzonetta

Dolce coninzamento
canto per la più fina
che sia, al mio parimento,
d'Agri infino in Mesina,
ciò è la più avenente: 5
«O stella rilucente
che levi la maitina!».
Quando m'apar davanti,
li suo' dolzi sembianti
mi 'ncendon la corina.   10

«Dolce meo sir, se 'ncendi,
or io che deggio fare?
Tu stesso mi riprendi,
se mi vei favellare,
ca tu m'ài 'namorata,   15
a lo cor m'ài lanciata,
sì ca difor non pare:
rimembriti a la fiata
quand'io t'ebi abrazzata
a li dolzi basciari».   20

Ed io basciando stava
in gran diletamento
con quella che m'amava,
bionda, viso d'argento.
Presente mi contava,   25
e non mi si celava,
tutto suo convenente;
e disse: «Ie t'ameraggio
e non ti falleraggio
a tutto 'l mio vivente.   30

17

I sing a sweet preamble
For the best of all,
Or so she seems to me,
I mean the loveliest,
From Agri to Messina: 5
"O star that shines so bright,
You who rise at dawn!"
When you come into view,
The sweetness of your looks
Sets my heart all aflame.   10

"Sweet lord, if you're on fire,
What am I now to do?
You chastise me yourself
If you should see me talk;
You made me fall in love   15
And pierced my heart straight through,
So outside it's not seen;
Remember well the time
When I embraced you fast
With kisses that were sweet."   20

And I kept kissing her
To my immense delight,
The one who loved me so,
The blonde, with radiant face.
She told me openly   25
All of her inner thoughts,
Concealing none from me,
And said: "I'll love but you
And never be untrue
As long as I shall live.   30

Al mio vivente, amore,
io non ti falliraggio
per lo lusingatore
che parla tal fallaggio,
ed io sì t'ameraggio   35
per quello ch'è salvaggio;
Dio li mandi dolore,
unqua non vegna a maggio:
tant'è di mal usaggio
che di stat'à gelore».   40

For all of life, my love,
I'll never be disloyal
Despite the slanderer
Alleging some betrayal,
And I shall love you still   35
Despite the one who's rude:
God grant he feels due pain
And fails to live till May:
His nature is so base
He's cold in summer too."   40

The Tenzoni

18a   Tenzone

Ai deo d'amore, a te faccio preghera
ca mi 'ntendiate s'io chero razone:
cad io son tutto fatto a tua manera,
aggio cavelli e barba a tua fazzone   4

ed ogni parte aio, viso e cera,
e seggio in quattro serpi ogni stagione;
per l'ali gran giornata m'è leggera,
son ben nato a tua isperagione.   8

E son montato per le quattro scale,
e som' asiso, ma tu m'ài feruto
de lo dardo de l'auro, ond'ò gran male,   11

che per mezzo lo core m'ài partuto:
di quello de lo piombo fo altretale
a quella per cui questo m'è avenuto.   14

18a Abbot of Tivoli

O god of Love, pray hear my plea
For justice I would seek from you:
For I am fashioned just like you,

And have a beard and hair like yours,   4
A face and look like yours as well,
And sit with four snakes at all times;
On wings I travel far with ease,
And took your likeness at my birth.   8

I have ascended all four steps
And rest at last, but I've been struck
By your gold dart, so I'm in pain,   11

For you have split my heart in two:
With your lead dart you've done the same
To her for whom I'm in this state.   14

18b   Tenzone

Feruto sono isvarïatamente:
Amore m'à feruto, or per che cosa?
Per ch'io vi saccia dir lo convenente
di quelli che del trovar no ànno posa,   4

ca dicono in lor ditto spessamente
ch'amore à in sé deïtate inclosa,
ed io sì dico che non è neiente,
ca più d'un dio non è né essere osa.   8

E chi lo mi volesse contastare,
io li lo mostreria per *quia* e quanto,
come non è più d'una deïtate.   11

In vanitate non voglio più stare:
voi che trovate novo ditto e canto,
partitevi da ciò, che voi peccate.   14

18b   Giacomo da Lentini

I have been wounded differently:
Love wounded me, but to what end?
So you may grasp the view of those
Who never cease to write of love   4

And often claim in poetry
That love contains divinity,
I do affirm that it does not,
For just one god exists, not more.   8

Should someone wish to disagree,
I'll demonstrate just how and why
There can be but one deity.   11

I do not wish to waste my time,
So you who write new verse and song,
Steer clear of this, lest you would sin.   14

18c   Tenzone

Qual om riprende altrui spessamente,
a le rampogne vene a le fiate;
per voi lo dico, amico, imprimamente,
ca non credo ca lealmente amiate.   4

Che s'Amor vi stringesse coralmente,
non parlereste per divinitate;
anzi voi credereste veramente
che elli avesse in sé gran potestate.   8

Per ciò ch'è di sì scura canoscenza,
che n'adiven come d'una bataglia:
chi stâ veder riprende chi combatte.   11

Quella ripresa non tegn'e' valenza:
chi accatta 'l mercato, sa che vaglia,
chi leva, sente più che quel che batte.   14

18c   Abbot of Tivoli

One who rebukes another frequently
Will sometimes run the risk of reprimand;
I state this first of all to you, my friend,
For I don't think your love is genuine.   4

For if in fact Love bound you earnestly
You would not speak so theologically,
But rather you would certainly believe
That he possessed great power by himself.   8

He is so difficult to understand,
Since the experience is like a war:
The one who watches chides the one who fights.   11

To reprimand this way's no proof of worth:
The buyer knows the value of what's sold,
Who lifts his arm hurts more than he who beats.   14

18d   Tenzone

Cotale gioco mai non fue veduto,
ch'aggio vercogna di dir ciò ch'io sento,
e dottone che non mi sia creduto,
però ch'ogn'om ne vive a scaltrimento;   4

pur uno poco sia d'amor feruto
sì si ragenza e fa suo parlamento,
e dice: «Donna, s'io non aggio aiuto,
io me 'nde moro, e fonne saramento».   8

Però gran noia mi fanno menzonieri,
sì 'mprontamente dicon lor menzogna,
ch'eo lo vero dirialo volontieri;   11

ma tacciolmi, che no mi sia vergogna,
ca d'onne parte amor ò '· pensieri
ed entra '· meve com'agua in ispogna.   14

18d   Giacomo da Lentini

A game like this has not been seen,
And so I shrink from speaking out
And fear that I won't be believed,
Since everyone is so astute.   4

Although but faintly struck by Love
He'll dress in style and frame a speech
And say: "My love, without your help,
I'll surely die, I swear it's true."   8

And that's why liars are nettlesome:
They tell their lies so brazenly
That I would gladly tell the truth.   11

But fearing shame, I'll hold my tongue,
For I abound with thoughts of love
That enter me as water does a sponge.   14

18e   Tenzone

Con vostro onore facciovi uno 'nvito,
ser Giacomo valente, a cui inchino:
lo vostro amor voria fermo e compito,
e per vostro amor ben amo Lentino.   4

Lo vostro detto, poi ch'io l'aggio adito,
più mi rischiara che l'air a·sereno.
Maggio infra li altri mesi è 'l più alorito,
per dolzi fior che spande egli è 'l più fino.   8

Ordunque a maggio asimigliato siete,
che spandete dolzi detti ed amorosi
più di nullo altro amador ch'omo saccia.   11

Ed io v'amo più che voi non credete:
se 'nver' di voi trovai detti noiosi,
riposomende a l'ora ch'a voi piaccia.   14

18e   Abbot of Tivoli

To honor you I send you this appeal,
My worthy Giacomo, to whom I bow:
I'd have your love be full and resolute,
And by my love for you I love Lentino.   4

Your poem, as soon as I had heard it read,
Makes me more cheerful than the clearest sky.
May is the most sweet-scented of all months,
The finest for the fragrant flowers it spreads.   8

Now, I compare you to the month of May,
Who spread the loveliest and sweetest poems
Of any lover one has ever known.   11

Indeed I love you more than you can know:
If I wrote irksome poems regarding you,
I will refrain so as to bring you joy.   14

19a   Tenzone

Solicitando un poco meo savere
e con lui mi vogliendo dilettare,
un dubio che mi misi ad avere
a voi lo mando per determinare.   4

On'omo dice ch'amor à potere
e li coraggi distringe ad amare,
ma eo no li lo voglio consentire,
però ch'amore no parse ni pare.   8

Ben trova l'omo una amorositate
la quale par che nasca di piacere,
e zo vol dire omo che sia amore;   11

eo no li saccio altra qualitate,
ma zo che è, da voi voglio audire:
però ven faccio sentenzïatore.   14

19a   Iacopo Mostacci

To stimulate my intellect
And take some pleasure in its use,
A crux that's given me some thought
I send to you to explicate.   4

All say that love possesses power
And forces every heart to love,
But I do not agree at all,
Since love's not been, nor can be, seen.   8

The poets write of sentiment
That seems engendered by delight,
And this, they say, means love exists.   11

What else it is I do not know,
But I would like to hear from you,
So I ask you to serve as judge.   14

19b   Tenzone

Però ch'Amore no si pò vedere
e no si tratta corporalemente,
manti ne son di sì folle sapere
che credeno ch'Amor sia nïente;   4

ma po' ch'Amore si face sentire
dentro dal cor signoreggiar la gente,
molto maggiore pregio deve avere
che se 'l vedessen visibilemente.   8

Per la vertute de la calamita
como lo ferro atra' no si vede,
ma sì lo tira signorevolmente;   11

e questa cosa a credere mi 'nvita
ch'Amore sia; e dàmi grande fede
che tutor sia creduto fra la gente.   14

19b   Pier de la Vigna

Because Love is not visible
And unlike matter can't be touched,
So many who are ignorant
Believe that love does not exist.   4

But since love can be felt to rule
Within the hearts of men, it should
Be granted greater consequence
Than if they saw it with their eyes.   8

One cannot see how iron is moved
By virtue of the lodestone's power,
Yet it's moved irresistibly;   11

And this is what induces me
To think that Love exists, and trust
That others likewise think so too.   14

19c   Tenzone

Amor è uno disio che ven da core
per abondanza di gran piacimento,
e li occhi imprima generan l'amore
e lo core li dà nutricamento.   4

Ben è alcuna fiata om amatore
senza vedere so 'namoramento,
ma quell'amor che stringe con furore
da la vista de li occhi à nascimento,   8

che li occhi rapresentan a lo core
d'onni cosa che veden bono e rio,
com'è formata naturalemente;   11

e lo cor, che di zo è concepitore,
imagina, e piace quel disio:
e questo amore regna fra la gente.   14

19c   Giacomo da Lentini

Love's a desire that issues from the heart
From an abundance of intense delight,
And first of all the eyes engender it
And then the heart provides it nourishment.   4

Indeed it's true that lovers sometimes fall
In love who've never seen their lady love,
But love that captivates with ardent zeal
Is brought to life from what the eyes have seen,   8

For it's the eyes that bring inside the heart
What they perceive, the good and bad alike,
And in the form that nature generates;   11

And afterward the heart, receiving it,
Conceives an image, and desire that pleases:
It is this love that rules throughout the world.   14

The Sonnets

20 Sonetto

Lo giglio quand'è colto tost'è passo,
da poi la sua natura lui no è giunta,
ed io dacunche son partuto un passo
da voi, mia donna, dolemi ogni giunta.   4

Per che d'amare ogni amadore passo,
in tante altezze lo mio core giunta:
così mi fere Amor là 'vunque passo,
com'aghila quand'a la caccia è giunta.   8

Oi lasso me, che nato fui in tal punto,
s'unque no amasse se non voi, chiù gente,
questo saccia madonna da mia parte.   11

Imprima che vi vidi ne fuo' punto,
servi'vi ed inora'vi a tutta gente,
da voi, bella, lo mio core non parte.   14

20

The lily fades as soon as it is picked,
Since it's no longer joined by nature's bond;
And when I'm parted from you for a spell,
My lady love, I ache in every joint.   4

Since every lover I surpass in love,
My heart ascends to great and lofty heights.
In every place I go Love strikes me hard,
Just like an eagle having caught its prey.   8

Unhappy me, born at a point in time
When I could love but you, most noble one,
And let my lady hear these words from me.   11

The instant I saw you I felt the blow,
I served you well and praised you everywhere,
My heart shall never part, my love, from you.   14

21   Sonetto

Sì come il sol che manda la sua spera
e passa per lo vetro e no lo parte,
e l'altro vetro che le donne spera,
che passa gli ochi e va da l'altra parte,   4

così l'Amore fere là ove spera
e mandavi lo dardo da sua parte:
fere in tal loco che l'omo non spera,
passa per gli ochi e lo core diparte.   8

Lo dardo de l'Amore là ove giunge,
da poi che dà feruta sì s'aprende
di foco ch'arde dentro e fuor non pare;   11

e due cori insemora li giunge,
de l'arte de l'amore sì gli aprende,
e face l'uno e l'altro d'amor pare.   14

21

Just like the sun that sends its rays
Through glass without fragmenting it,
Or ladies' mirrored images
Pass through the eyes and go beyond,   4

So Love will strike where he intends
And send his dart from where he stands:
It strikes the place that's least foreseen,
Goes through the eyes and cleaves the heart.   8

The place where Love's dart comes to rest
Flames up as soon as it is struck
And burns within, unseen without;   11

And it joins two hearts into one
And teaches them the art of love:
Each loves the other equally.   14

22   Sonetto

Or come pote sì gran donna entrare
per gli ochi mei che sì piccioli sone?
e nel mio core come pote stare,
che 'nentr'esso la porto laonque i' vone?   4

Lo loco là onde entra già non pare,
ond'io gran meraviglia me ne dòne;
ma voglio lei a lumera asomigliare,
e gli ochi mei al vetro ove si pone.   8

Lo foco inchiuso poi passa di fore
lo suo lostrore, sanza far rotura,
così per gli ochi mi pass'a lo core,   11

no la persona, ma la sua figura:
rinovellare mi voglio d'amore,
poi porto insegna di tal crïatura.   14

22

How can so great a lady pass
Straight through my eyes, which are so small?
And in my heart how can she dwell,
Borne there by me wherever I should go?   4

The place she enters stays unseen,
Which puts me in a state of awe;
But I'd compare her to a light,
My eyes the glass on which it strikes.   8

The fire's light then passes through
Outside, no rupture being made:
Just so she goes through my eyes to my heart,   11

Not her body, but her image.
My love's renewed because I bear
The likeness of her mortal being.   14

23 Sonetto

Molti amadori la lor malatia
portano in core, che 'n vista non pare,
ed io non posso sì celar la mia,
ch'ella non paia per lo mio penare,   4

però che son sotto altrui segnoria,
né di meve nonn-ò neiente a·ffare,
se non quanto madonna mia voria,
ch'ella mi pote morte e vita dare.   8

Su' è lo core e suo son tutto quanto,
e chi non à consiglio da suo core,
non vive infra la gente como deve,   11

cad io non sono mio né più né tanto,
se non quanto madonna vede fore
e uno poco di spirito ch'è 'n meve.   14

23

Many lovers bear their malady
Inside their hearts, where it cannot be seen,
Yet I'm unable to conceal my own
So that it's not revealed by my distress,   4

For I am held beneath another's rule,
And cannot act according to my will,
Except for what my Lady might desire,
For she decides if I shall live or die.   8

My heart is hers, and all of me as well,
And he who doesn't listen to his heart
Cannot consort with others as he should,   11

For I am not myself, except for what
My lady sees outside of me
And just a bit of spirit left inside.   14

24   Sonetto

Donna, vostri sembianti mi mostraro
isperanza d'amore e benvolenza,
ed io sovr'ogni gioia lo n'ò caro
lo vostro amore e far vostra piagenza.   4

Or vi mostrate irata, dunqu'è raro
senza ch'io pechi darmi penitenza,
e fatt'avete de la penna caro,
come nochier ch'à falsa canoscenza.   8

Disconoscenza – ben mi par che sia,
la conoscenza – che nonn-à fermezze,
che si rimuta per ogni volere;   11

dunque non siete voi in vostra balia,
né inn-altrui ch'aia ferme prodezze,
e non avrete bon fine al gioire.   14

24

My lady, your expressions raised in me
The hope of gaining love and your good will,
And I hold dear above all other joys
Your love and doing what most pleases you.   4

But now you seem annoyed, so it is strange
That I, not having sinned, should make amends,
While you have seldom put your sail to use,
Just like a skipper who's incompetent.   8

I really think it's ignorance,
A knowledge lacking steadiness
That varies with each new caprice;   11

So you aren't master of yourself
Nor of one in whom virtue's firm,
And you won't find true happiness.   14

25 Sonetto

Ogn'omo c'ama de' amar so 'nore
e de la donna che prende ad amare,
e foll'è chi non è soferitore,
che la natura – de' omo isforzare,   4

e non de' dire ciò ch'egli àve in core,
che la parola non pò ritornare:
da tutta gente tenut'è migliore
chi à misura – ne lo so parlare.   8

Dunque, madonna, mi voglio sofrire
di far sembianti a la vostra contrata,
che la gente si sforza di maldire;   11

però lo faccio, non siate blasmata,
che l'omo si diletta più di dire
lo male che lo bene a la fïata.   14

25

A lover must protect his name
As well as hers whose love he chose,
And he is mad who lacks restraint
For he must curb his natural bent,   4

And must not say what's in his heart,
Since what is said can't be unsaid:
The one all hold to be the best
Embraces measure when he speaks.   8

And so, my lady, I'll refrain
From glancing toward you when we meet,
Since people try hard to malign;   11

I do this so you won't be blamed,
For some at times take more delight
In slandering than giving praise.   14

26 Sonetto

A l'aire claro ò vista ploggia dare,
ed a lo scuro rendere clarore;
e foco arzente ghiaccia diventare,
e freda neve rendere calore;   4

e dolze cose molto amareare,
e de l'amare rendere dolzore;
e dui guerreri infin a pace stare,
e 'ntra dui amici nascereci errore.   8

Ed ò vista d'Amor – cosa più forte,
ch'era feruto e sanòmi ferendo,
lo foco donde ardea stutò con foco;   11

la vita che mi dè fue la mia morte,
lo foco che mi stinse ora ne 'ncendo,
d'amor mi trasse e misemi in su' loco.   14

26

On clear days I have seen it rain,
And I've seen darkness flash with light,
And likewise lightning turn to hail,
And frozen snow engender heat;   4

And sweet things taste of bitterness,
And what is bitter taste most sweet;
Two enemies make peace at last,
And discord grow between two friends.   8

Yet stranger things I've seen of Love,
Who healed my wounds by wounding me;
The fire in me he quenched with fire.   11

The life he gave me was my death;
The fire that slew me burns once more,
Once saved from love, I'm seized anew.   14

27 Sonetto

Io m'aggio posto in core a Dio servire,
com'io potesse gire in paradiso,
al santo loco ch'aggio audito dire,
o' si mantien sollazzo, gioco e riso.   4

Sanza mia donna non vi voria gire,
quella ch'à blonda testa e claro viso,
che sanza lei non poteria gaudere,
estando da la mia donna diviso.   8

Ma no lo dico a tale intendimento
perch'io pecato ci vellesse fare,
se non veder lo suo bel portamento   11

e lo bel viso e 'l morbido sguardare:
che 'l mi teria in gran consolamento,
veggendo la mia donna in ghiora stare.   14

27

I've set my heart on serving God
So I might go to Paradise,
That holy place, as I have heard,
Where all is laughter, fun, and games.   4

I would not go without my love,
Whose face is bright and hair is blond,
For without her I'd have no joy,
Deprived of her companionship.   8

Yet I do not intend for this
To signify I wish to sin,
But just to see her gracious mien,   11

Her lovely face, and kind regard:
For it would bring me great delight
To see my love in glory's realm.   14

28   Sonetto

Lo viso – mi fa andare alegramente,
lo bello viso – mi fa rinegare;
lo viso – me conforta ispesamente,
l'adorno viso – che mi fa penare.   4

Lo chiaro viso – de la più avenente,
l'adorno viso, – riso – me fa fare:
di quello viso – parlane la gente,
che nullo viso – a viso – li pò stare.   8

Chi vide mai così begli ochi in viso,
né sì amorosi fare li sembianti,
né boca con cotanto dolce riso?   11

Quand'eo li parlo moroli davanti,
e paremi ch'i' vada in paradiso,
e tegnomi sovrano d'ogn'amante.   14

28

Her face suffuses me with joy,
Her lovely face makes me recant;
Her face consoles me constantly,
Her pretty face which brings me pain.   4

The bright face of who's loveliest,
Her pretty face, prompts me to smile:
Of that face all the people speak,
No other face can brook compare.   8

Whoever saw such lovely eyes
On any face, such loving looks,
Or mouth with such a charming smile?   11

But when I talk with her I die
And seem to go to paradise,
And deem myself, in love, supreme.   14

29 Sonetto

Eo viso – e son diviso – da lo viso,
e per aviso – credo ben visare;
però diviso – "viso" – da lo "viso",
ch'altr'è lo viso – che lo divisare.   4

E per aviso – viso – in tale viso
de lo qual me non posso divisare:
viso – a vedere quell'è peraviso,
che no è altro se non Deo divišare.   8

Entro a viso – e peraviso – no è diviso,
che non è altro che visare in viso:
però mi sforzo tuttor a visare.   11

E credo per aviso – che da "viso"
giamai me' non pos'essere diviso,
che l'uomo vi 'nde possa divisare.   14

29

I see, but only from afar, her face,
Yet in my mind I think I see her well;
This image I distinguish from her face,
For seeing differs from imagining.   4

Her image I project within my mind,
From which I can't dissociate myself.
To see her face puts me in paradise,
And that is but to contemplate our Lord.   8

No breach between her face and paradise,
Which is the same as gazing at her face:
That's why I always strive to look at it.   11

And I am led by reason to believe
I never will be parted from that face,
Whatever others think in this regard.   14

30 Sonetto

Sì alta amanza à pres'a lo me' core,
ch'i' mi disfido de lo compimento:
che in aguila gruera ò messo amore
ben èst'orgoglio, ma no falimento,   4

ch'Amor l'encalza e spera aulente frore,
ch'albor altera incrina dolce vento,
e lo diamante rompe a tutte l'ore
de lacreme lo molle sentimento.   8

Donqua, madonna, se lacrime e pianto
de lo diamante frange le durezze,
vostre altezze poria isbasare   11

lo meo penar amoroso ch'è tanto,
umilïare le vostre durezze,
foco d'amor in vui, donna, alumare.   14

30

A love so noble seized my heart
That I despair of its success:
To choose to love a bird of prey
May come from pride, but not from fault,   4

For Love will prod it and bestir
The fragrant flower, a gentle breeze
Will bend a lofty tree, soft tears
Will always cut the diamond's rough.   8

So, Lady, if my tears and plaint
Can crack the diamond's stoniness,
The pain of love that burdens me   11

Might moderate your arrogance,
Make you subdue your stoniness,
And, Lady, light the fire of love in you.   14

31 Sonetto

Per sofrenza si vince gran vetoria
ond'omo ven spesora in dignitate,
sì con' si trova ne l'antica istoria
di Iobo ch'ebbe tanta aversitate,   4

chi fu sofrent'e no perdeo memoria
per grave pene ch'a lui fosser date,
onde fu data corona ne la groria
davanti la divina maiestate.   8

Però conforto grande di zo prendo:
ancor la mia ventura vada torta
no me dispero certo malamente,   11

che la ventura sempre va corendo
e tostamente rica gioia aporta
a chïunque n'è bono soferente.   14

31

Through patience great success is won
That often brings a man renown,
As we find in the ancient tale
Of Job who met with much adversity,   4

Who suffered and still kept his head
Despite the heavy pain he bore;
A crown of glory was his gift,
Bestowed in front of God, His Lord.   8

By this I'm greatly comforted:
Although my luck could turn awry
I surely will not court despair,   11

For Fortune's wheel turns round and round
And quickly brings some precious joy
To those who suffer patiently.   14

32   Sonetto

Certo me par che far dea bon signore
i·signoria sua fier cominciamento,
sì che lo doti chi à malvagìa in core,
e chi l'à bon, megliori il su' talento.   4

Così poria venire 'n grande onore
e a bon fin de lo so reggimento,
che sed al cominciar mostr'amarore,
porase render dolce al finimento.   8

Ma in te, Amore, – veggio lo contraro,
sì como quello pien di falisone,
ch'al cominciar no mostri fior d'amaro;   11

poi scruopi tua malvagia openïone,
qual più ti serve a fé, quel men ài caro,
ond'eo t'aprovo per signor felone.   14

32

It seems quite clear a noble lord should base
His rule at first on forcefulness,
So that he's feared by men of evil will
And those whose will is good may strengthen it.   4

In doing so he might achieve great fame
And bring a happy end to his regime,
For if he starts by acting ruthlessly,
He still can end his rule by being kind.   8

But, Love, in you I find the opposite,
Like someone who is full of perfidy,
Since at the start you don't at all seem rank,   11

Then down the road you bare your evil hand:
You're least endeared to those who serve you best,
So I declare you lord of treachery.   14

33 Sonetto

Sì como 'l parpaglion ch'à tal natura
non si rancura – de ferire al foco,
m'avete fatto, gentil crëatura,
non date cura, – s'eo incendo e coco.   4

Venendo a voi lo meo cor s'asigura
pensando tal chiarura – sï'a gioco:
come 'l zitello e' oblio l'arsura,
mai non trovai ventura – in alcun loco.   8

Ciò è lo cor, che no à ciò che brama,
se mor ardendo ne la dolce fiamma,
rendendo vita come la finise;   11

e poi l'amor naturalmente il chiama,
e l'adornezze ch'ensperie l'afiama,
rendendo vita come la finise.   14

33

Just as the butterfly in nature's grasp
Does not recoil from rushing into fire,
You've forced me to react, my noble one,
And do not care if I catch fire and burn.   4

Approaching you, my heart is reassured
Believing such bright light is meant for play:
For like a child I overlook the heat,
But then I've never had good luck at all.   8

I mean the heart, not having what it wants,
Must die by burning in the lovely flame,
To end its life just as the phoenix does;   11

Then love by nature calls it back to life,
And beauty raining down provides it warmth,
Restoring it to life when all is done.   14

34 Sonetto

Chi non avesse – mai veduto foco
no crederia che cocere potesse,
anti li sembraria solazzo e gioco
lo so isprendore, quando lo vedesse.   4

Ma s'ello lo tocasse in alcun loco,
be·li sembrara che forte cocesse:
quello d'Amore m'à tocato un poco,
molto me coce, Deo, che s'aprendesse!   8

Che s'aprendesse – in voi, donna mia,
che mi mostrate dar solazzo amando,
e voi mi date pur pen'e tormento.   11

Certo l'Amore fa gran vilania,
che no distringe te che vai gabando,
a me che servo non dà isbaldimento.   14

34

If one had never seen a flame of fire
He wouldn't think that it could ever burn,
So after having seen its radiance
He'd think that it was meant for fun and games.   4

But if he were to touch it here or there,
He'd think it burned with great intensity:
The flame of Love has touched me just a bit
And burns me badly – God, if love could blaze!   8

If love could only blaze in you, my fair,
Who make me think you bring the joy of love,
Yet bring me only anguish and distress.   11

Assuredly Love acts with disrespect,
Allowing you to play me for a fool:
To me, who serves, he brings no joy at all.   14

35 Sonetto

Diamante, né smiraldo, né zafino,
né vernul'altra gema prezïosa,
topazzo, né giaquinto, né rubino,
né l'aritropia, ch'è sì vertudiosa,   4

né l'amatisto, né 'l carbonchio fino,
lo qual è molto risprendente cosa,
non àno tante belezze in domino
quant'à in sé la mia donna amorosa.   8

E di vertute tutte l'autre avanza,
e somigliante al sole è di sprendore,
co la sua conta e gaia inamoranza,   11

e più bell'è che rosa e che frore:
Cristo le doni vita ed alegranza,
e sì l'acresca in gran pregio ed onore.   14

35

No diamond, sapphire, emerald,
Nor any other precious stone,
No topaz, zircon, any ruby,
Nor heliotrope, all-powerful,   4

Nor amethyst, nor perfect garnet,
A gem that shines with brilliancy,
Possesses beauty that's as great
As has my loving lady fair.   8

For she excels in virtue all,
And shines just like the sun above,
With dignified and joyous love,   11

And is more lovely than a rose.
May Christ grant her long life and joy,
And multiply her worth and fame.   14

36 Sonetto

Madonna à 'n sé vertute con valore
più che nul'altra gemma prezïosa,
che isguardando mi tolse lo core,
cotant'è di natura vertudiosa.   4

Più luce sua beltate e dà sprendore
che non fa 'l sole né null'autra cosa,
de tutte l'autre ell'è sovran'e frore,
che nulla apareggiare a lei non osa.   8

Di nulla cosa – non à mancamento
né fu ned è né non serà sua pare,
né 'n cui si trovi tanto complimento;   11

e credo ben, se Dio l'avesse a fare,
non vi metrebbe sì su' 'ntendimento
che la potesse simile formare.   14

36

My lady's virtue and her worth
No precious gem can emulate;
Her nature is so powerful
She seized my heart with just a glance.   4

Her beauty shines and yields more light
Than does the sun or anything;
Of all she is supreme, the best,
No lady dares compete with her.   8

She has no fault of any kind
Nor any peer, nor ever had,
Nor will, such is her flawlessness;   11

I think if God had it to do,
He could not so engage his thought
As to create one just like her.   14

37   Sonetto

Angelica figura – e comprobata,
dobiata – di ricura – e di grandezze,
di senno e d'adornezze – sete ornata
e nata – d'afinata – gentilezze.   4

Non mi parete femina incarnata,
ma fatta – per gli frori di belezze
in cui tutta vertudie è divisata,
e data – voi tutt'è avenantezze.   8

In voi è pregio, senno e conoscenza,
e sofrenza, – ch'è somma de li bene,
como la spene – che fiorisc'e ingrana: 11

come lo nome, aut'è la potenza
di dar sentenza – chi contra voi viene,
sì com'avene – a la città romana.   14

37

Angelic figure manifest,
Endowed twofold with wealth and worth,
You are adorned with sense and charm
And born to high nobility.   4

You seem no woman made of flesh,
But bred of flowers' loveliness
In which all virtue is displayed,
Together with attractiveness.   8

In you are merit, wisdom, sense,
And patience too, the greatest good,
Like hope that blooms and flourishes: 11

And like your name, you wield the power
To judge whoever flouts your will,
As happens at the court of Rome.   14

38 Sonetto

Quand'om à un bon amico leiale
cortesemente il de' saper tenere,
e no·l de' trar sì cort'o delïale
che si convegna per forza partire.   4

Che d'aquistar l'amico poco vale,
da poi che no lo sa ben mantenere,
che lo de' conoscere bene e male,
donare e torre, e saperl'agradire.   8

Ma molti creden tenere amistade
sol per pelare altrui a la cortese,
e non mostrare in vista ciò che sia;   11

be·lli falla pensieri in veritate,
chi crede fare d'altrui borsa spese,
ch'omo vivente sofrir no·l poria.   14

38

When someone has a true and loyal friend
He must know how to treat him worthily
And not become so brusque or so untrue
That parting ways would be the better course.   4

For it would make no sense to gain a friend
If one did not know how to keep his trust:
One has to know his good side and his bad,
And how to give and take, and how to please.   8

But many think a friendship serves the end
Of fleecing others through false courtesy
And not revealing what it is you've done.   11

The one who hopes to spend with others' wealth
Indeed reveals a lack of common sense,
For there's no living soul who'd stand for it.   14

The Lyrics of Dubious Authorship

39 Canzone

Membrando l'amoroso dipartire,
com'eo partivi di voi, donna mia,
ch'a piè basciando i' vi diceva «a Deo»,
sì forte mi combatton li sospire
pur aspetando, bella, quella dia,   5
com'eo ritorni a voi, dolze amor meo;
sì languisco eo,
    madonna, pur pensando
e disïando
   com'eo mi torni a voi,   10
sì ca noi dui
    viviamo in gio' basciando.

La ragione è lo dolze parlamento
che tu dicevi a me, bella, in parvenza,
lo giorno ch'eo da voi mi dipartivi: 15
«Se vai, amore, me lasci in tormento;
io n'averò pensiero e cordoglienza
e disïo sol di venire a tevi.
Sì come audivi
   che vai lontana parte,   20
da me si parte
   la gioia del meo core;
se vai, amore,
    lo meo cor lasci in parte».

Lo mio gire, amorosa, ben sacciate,   25
mi fa contravolere in tutte guise:
a voi ritornar gran disiro aio,
ma lo meo sire, che m'à in potestate,
a lo 'nconinciamento l'impromise,
di ritornare a Lentino di maio.   30

39   (Authorship dubious)

Remembering my loving fond farewell
As I took leave of you, my lady love,
And kneeling at your feet bade you "Adieu,"
I am completely overcome by sighs
Anticipating, my beloved, the day   5
When I'll return to you, my dearest one;
I languish,
            lady, for I always think
And yearn
            about when I'll return to you,   10
For both of us
            to live and kiss in joy.

The reason is the sweetness of the words
You spoke to me, my fair, quite openly,
The day that I was taking leave of you: 15
"If you depart, my love, I'll be distraught;
I'll be in agony and deep distress
And my sole wish will be to come to you.
Because I've heard
            you're going far away,   20
The joy inside my heart
                abandons me;
If you should leave,
            my love, you'll cleave my heart."

My departure, you well know, my fair,   25
Leaves me dissatisfied in every way;
My fondest wish is to return to you,
However, he who holds me in his power,
My master, promised me right at the start
That to Lentino he'd return in May.   30

Lo meo coraio
   d'altro non si diletta,
tutora aspetta
    che con voi si soggiorni,
in gioia ritorni   35
     la pena ch'io sento.

Certo, madonna mia, non so' alungato,
[...] ma ciascuna dia
mi par ch'i' sia di voi più disïoso;
poi che 'l corpo dimori in altro lato,   40
lo cor con voi soggiorna tutavia,
e io ne so' alegro e vivone gioioso,
de l'amoroso
    rimembrare ch'io faccio,
quando in braccio   45
     io vi tenia basciando,
adomandando
    lo comiato in sollaccio.

Tanta baldanza in disïo tenente
e' no creo che sia in alcuno amante,   50
né aggia in sua intendanza, al mio parere,
quant'e' in privanza teno spessamente
e da me sì non tolle e parte, mante
fïate in braccio voi mi par tenere,
a ciò avere   55
   vedere sì soniando,
lo giorno quando
    vorei fossimo i·loco
ched i' tal foco
    ramortasse mortando.   60

My heart
      finds happiness in this alone,
And waits
      unceasingly to dwell with you
And have the pain   35
        I feel turned into joy.

Indeed, my lady, I won't be away,
… but every day
I seem to long for you more ardently;
And though my body dwells elsewhere,   40
My heart resides continually with you,
And I am happy and I live in joy
Recalling
      such fond memories of when
I held you   45
      in my arms while kissing you,
Most pleasantly
      requesting leave of you.

I do not think that any lover is
So wholly self-assured of his desire,   50
Nor is so dedicated, in my view,
As I am often while I'm far away;
And I'm not so removed and kept apart
That I don't seem to hold you in my arms,
And having that   55
      by seeing in my dreams
The day when
      I wish we were where
I might put out
      the fire I once put out.   60

40 Sonetto

Lo badalisco a lo specchio lucente
traggi'a morire con isbaldimento,
lo cesne canta più gioiosamente
da ch'egli è presso a lo suo finimento,   4

lo paon turba istando più gaudente
quand'ai suoi piedi fa riguardamento,
l'augel fenice s'arde veramente
per ritornare a novel nascimento;   8

a·ttai nature sentom'abenuto,
ch'a morte vado allegro a le bellezze,
e forzo 'l canto presso a lo finire,   11

estando gaio torno dismaruto,
ardendo in foco 'novo in allegrezze:
per voi, più gente, a cui spero redire.   14

41 Sonetto

Guardando basalisco velenoso
che 'l so isguardare face l'om perire,
e l'aspido, serpente invidïoso,
che per ingegno mette altrui a morire,   4

e lo dragone, ch'è sì argoglioso,
cui elli prende no lassa partire;
a loro asemblo l'amor ch'è doglioso,
che tormentando altrui fa languire.   8

In ciò à natura l'amor veramente,
che in u·guardar conquide lo coraggio
e per ingegno lo fa star dolente,   11

e per orgoglio mena grande oltraggio:
cui ello prende grave pena sente
e gran tormento ch'à su' signoraggio.   14

40   (Authorship dubious)

Before a shiny mirror the basilisk
Crawls to its death with joyfulness,
The swan will sing most blissfully
When lying at the brink of death,   4

The peacock, when it's happiest,
Is ruffled looking at its feet,
The phoenix sets itself on fire
To come back and be born again;   8

I feel a kinship with these animals
Because for beauty I meet death with cheer
And sing more ardently close to the end,   11

And feeling merry I grow sad,
And burning I'm restored to joy, for you,
Most noble one, to whom I would return.   14

41   (Authorship dubious)

Looking at the deadly basilisk
Whose gaze can cause the death of any man,
And at the asp, a snake that's envious,
Which uses guile to kill its enemies,   4

And at the dragon, so puffed up with pride
It will not free the prey it has ensnared;
To them I liken love that's full of pain,
Whose torture causes one to waste away.   8

Love's nature truly does consist in this:
A single look can subjugate the heart
And its deceitfulness bring misery,   11

And its disdain engender great offense:
All those it seizes suffer grievously
And those it masters live in agony.   14

Notes to the Poems

The Italian text of Giacomo da Lentini's lyrics and all critical citations are taken from the edition and commentary of Roberto Antonelli published in *I poeti della Scuola siciliana. Vol. 1. Giacomo da Lentini* (Milan: Mondadori, 2008). His text comprises 41 lyrics, 38 whose authorship is certain, and 3 of doubtful authenticity. The majority of compositions are sonnets (21), all of which employ the same *abab abab* rhyme scheme in the octave. Two schemes are used in the sestet, *cde cde*, and, less frequently, *cdc dcd*. The metrical scheme accompanying the note for each lyric adheres to the following format: an upper case letter represents an eleven-syllable verse (*endecasillabo*), a lower case letter a seven-syllable verse (*settenario*); a subscript is used to indicate the number of syllables of any other verse; patterns of internal rhyme are contained within parentheses and precede the verse rhyme. Indications of inter-stanzaic properties adopt the nomenclature of Occitan poetry: *coblas capfinidas* signifies that the last rhyme word of a stanza reappears in the first line of the following stanza; *coblas unissonans*, that the same rhyme scheme and same rhyme sounds recur in all stanzas; *coblas singulars* that in every stanza the rhyme scheme never changes while the rhyme sounds differ; *coblas doblas*, that the rhyme scheme never changes but the rhyme sounds differ every two stanzas.

1
My lady, I wish to tell you
Canzone of five stanzas *singulars*, sixteen verses each:
abaC dbdC eef(f)G hhi(i)G

Among Giacomo's most celebrated lyrics, this canzone is based on a translation of a part of the Occitan *canso* "A vos, midontç, voill retrair' en cantan," by Folquet de Marselha. In the *De vulgari eloquentia* (2.6.6), Dante cites Folquet's *canso* "Tant m'abellis l'amoros pessamens" as representative of the highest level of rhetorical eloquence in Occitan poetry.

27 *La salamandra audivi*: According to medieval bestiaries, the salamander had the power to survive in fire without being burned by its flames, making it an ideal metaphor for the nature of love, which burned like fire without consuming the lover.

32 *My wheat sprouts ears, and yet no seed takes root*: A metaphor expressing the thought that the poet's love, unreciprocated by his lady, has not come to fruition.

2
Extraordinarily
Canzonetta of seven stanzas *singulars*, nine verses each;
coblas capfinidas between stanzas 1 & 2 and 4 & 5:
abc abc ddc

The remarkable initial verse of this celebrated lyric, "Meravigliosamente," containing only a single, long word of seven syllables, aptly expresses the poet-lover's exuberant, unrestrained adoration of his lady. The poem is called a *canzonetta* rather than a canzone because it employs the shorter *settenario* verse form rather than the hendecasyllable.

8 *For in my heart I bear / The portrait of your form*: The conceit of painting the image of the beloved and concealing it in the heart will be imitated by later poets in the vernacular, including Dante.

62 *"Your love, which is so dear, / Vouchsafe the Notary, / A native of Lentino"*: Giacomo's signature in the envoi of this *canzonetta* attests to the lyric's authenticity. Lentini is a small town near the eastern coast of Sicily.

3

I hope for recompense
Canzone of four stanzas *singulars*, fourteen verses each:
$a_8a_8b_4 \, c_8c_8b_4$; ded(e)F ghg(h)F

The poet traditionally seeks some form of recompense or reward
for the love he expresses for his lady in his poetry, which is meant to
honor her beauty, worthiness, and social superiority. The nature of
the reward is at times left vague, but in Giacomo's lyrics it consists of
receiving the lady's pity as a form of solace for the poet's emotional
tribulations. The poet here appeals to the lady to abandon her attitude
of arrogance, the chief impediment to his happiness since it prevents
her from expressing pity for his plight. His aspirations are buoyed by
steadfast hope alone. The four stanzas depict an increasing sense of
urgency on the part of the lover to prevail against the lady's resistence,
for ultimately his life, he says, hangs in the balance: *My fair, don't let me
die* (43). While he realizes he is speaking metaphorically, he employs the
language of desperation as a way of overpowering the lady's attitude of
sustained defiance. To drive home his point, he ends with the words
I'm destroyed (56).

4

Love will not let me seek
Canzone of five stanzas *singulars*, ten octosyllabic verses each; *capfinidas*
between stanzas 3 & 4: abab ccd eed

The lyric exploits the topos of the lover's expectation of pity ("merzede" or "pïetanza") as a reward for his love service by undermining it.
Since receiving the gift of pity is every lover's goal, this lover, surpris-
ingly, defies tradition and hopes that his novel approach will gain him
an advantage with his lady. The lyric proceeds by repeatedly justifying
such an approach by referring to norms that have undergone change
over time, until the theme is turned on its head in the last stanza.
Conclusion: Since he is able to change, she must also change, or he
will die.

In verse 17, the terms "merzede" and "pïetanza" are virtually synony-
mous, both signifying pity, sympathy, or mercy, although "merzede"
comprises a broader range of meaning that includes the notions of
recompense, reward, help, and courtesy. I render the terms variously
throughout Giacomo's poetry according to metrical constraints.

5

From my heart flows

"Discordo" of 176 verses from three to eleven syllables, in eleven stanzas of varying length:

I	1–18	$a_6(a_6)b_9 \ a_6(a_6)b_9 \ a_6(a_6)b_9; \ c_6c_6d_6(d_6)e_9 \ f_6f_6g_6(g_6)e_9 \ h_6h_6i_6(i_6)e_9$
II	19–34	$a_5a_5a_5b_5 \ b_5c_6c_5d_6; \ e_5e_5e_5f_5 \ f_5g_6g_5d_6; \ h_5h_5h_5i_5 \ i_5l_6l_5d_6$
III	35–51	$a_5b_6c_5 \ a_5b_6c_5 \ a_5b_6c_5$
IV	52–63	$a_5a_6b_5(f_5)c_8 \ d_5d_6b_5(f_5)c_8 \ e_5e_6b_5(f_5)c_8$
V	64–75	$(a_4)a_8b_6 \ (c_4)c_8b_6; \ (d_4)d_8e_6 \ (f_4)f_8e_6; \ (g_4)g_8h_6 \ (i_4)i_8h_6$
VI	76–94	$(a_4a_3)a_{10}b_6, \ (c_4c_3)c_{10}b_6; \ (d_4d_3)d_{10}e_6, \ [(f_4f_3)f_{10}e_6]; \ (g_4g_3)g_{10}h_6,$ $(i_4i_3)i_{10}h_6; \ (h_3)$llllll
VII	95–106	$(a_4)a_8b_6 \ (c_4)c_8b_6; \ (d_4)d_8e_6 \ (f_4)f_8e_6; \ (g_4)g_8h_6 \ (i_4)i_8h_6$
VIII	107–122	aaaa, bbbb, cccc; c_4cc_4c
IX	123–133	$a_5a_3a_3, \ b_6b_4b_4b_8, \ c_6d_4c_4d_8$
X	134–157	$(l_3)a_5(l_3)a(m_3)a_5(m_4)a; \ (a_3)b_6b_4b_4; \ c_6c_5c_4; \ d_4d_4e_4e_4f_4[f_4][g_4]$ $g_8; \ h_4h_4i_6h_4h_4i_8$
XI	158–176	aaab$_6$ cccb$_6$; $(b_4)d_8d_8$ddd$_8$; $(d_5)E(e_5)F \ (f_5)E(e_5)F; \ (f_4)g(g_3)G$

The lyric takes the form of a "discordo," a genre of canzone first appearing in Old French and Occitan poetry ("descort"), but which is rarely employed by early Italian poets. It is characterized by the use of stanzaic and metrical irregularities (e.g., stanzas of different length), short verses, and contrasting melodic and rhythmic elements within stanzas.

6

The passionate desire

Canzone of six stanzas *unissonans*, eight verses each; *capfinidas* between stanzas 1 & 2, 2 & 3, 3 & 4, and 5 & 6:
$(c_5)a_9b_9b_9a_9 \ c_9d_9d_5C$

The first four verses have generated a good deal of disagreement about their exact meaning. Nevertheless, the general idea appears to be that the poet-lover continues to lack recompense for his love, which requires him to take ever-greater risks in courting his lady.

7
A sense of anguish has come over me
Canzone of five stanzas *unissonans*, eight verses each:
A(a$_5$)BA(a$_5$)B (b$_5$)CCDD

Antonelli (179) cites Salvatore Santangelo's argument assigning the composition of the lyric to 1234 on the basis of political references contained in the fifth stanza.

> 32 *Exceeding measure, unlike humbleness*: The lady's pride has become excessive, passing beyond the limit of the golden mean, while humility does not. Therefore she should adopt an attitude of humility and offer him her sympathy.

> 34 *Like Florence, which behaves with arrogance*: Florence and Milan were hostile to the political ambitions of emperor Frederick II, while Pisa was sympathetic.

> 38 *You're like Milan with its war chariot*: Milan's "carroccio" was a large war chariot that bore the military standard of the city. Some critics interpret this reference as an allusion to the battle of Cortenuova (1237), in which the imperial forces of Frederick II seized the chariot, which symbolized Milan's opposition to willing submission to the monarchy. But the reference may be general and serve simply to qualify the lady's extraordinary power to dominate the poet-lover through pride.

8
My Love, I suffer and don't know how hope
Canzone of five stanzas *singulars*, ten verses each:
A(a$_5$)BC(c$_5$)B Dde eFF

> 34 *A lion is by instinct so disposed*: The lion's compassion before a humble opponent conceding defeat is a topos in medieval literature. It appears, for example, in Bertrand de Born's "Ar ve la coindeta sazos," Chiaro Davanzati's "La mia vita, poi [ch'è] sanza conforto," and possibly also Tomaso da Faenza's "Spesso di gioia."

9

Too long have I resided
Canzone of five *coblas doblas*, twelve verses each:
abC abC def def

The poem exploits the topos of *amor de lonh*, or love from afar, in
which the poet-lover regrets his folly in becoming separated from his
lady and expresses his desire to summon the courage to return to her.

   1 *Too long have I resided*: This incipit is based on the poem "Trop ai
   estat mon Bon Esper no vi" (I have not seen my Good Hope for too
   long a time) by the troubadour poet Perdigon, who flourished in
   Provence during the period 1190–1220.

11

Frequently an amorous desire
Canzone of five stanzas *singulars*, twelve verses each;
capfinidas between stanzas 1 & 2 and 2 & 3:
Aa$_5$B Aa$_5$B Cc$_5$d dEE

   10 *I could remain impaired*: His fear might cause him to continue
   remaining silent, which would prevent him from being able to
   resolve his dilemma.

12

In loving for so long
Canzone of five stanzas *singulars*, fourteen verses each:
capfinidas between stanzas 1 & 2, 2 & 3, and 3 & 4
abb(b$_5$)A abb(b$_5$)A c$_9$d(d$_5$)C cEE

The poet-lover confronts his lady's refusal to accept his love, despite
his praise of her. He wants to know how much she values his love,
and fears she loves him too little. Consequently his love entails much
suffering, and her pride, an aspect of her beauty, only increases it, for
"*pride's not bliss*" (41). The opening stanza's expression of the poet-lover's
quandary of not knowing how much the lady values his love, "*I wish that I
could see / The time when you'd be pleased / By what I'm worth to you, my worthy
one*" (2–4), finds reinforcement at the beginning of the last stanza: "*I
don't know how I seem to you*" (57); but he raises the stakes by informing
her that there is a limit to his waiting for her to respond to his desires,
which is death: "*But you will find me dead / If you won't have me in your
custody*" (63–4). This climax is immediately followed, and softened,

by an appeal to her, by means of exhortation, to reward his efforts with an expression of pity, which will cause in him the release of tears of happiness. Throughout this lyric, the poet-lover vacillates, as he does here, between opposing expressions of praise and criticism of his beloved. The first stanza closes on a negative note, the poet-lover's love anguish: "*witness how my heart is full of pain*" (14). Yet that pain, he says at the beginning of the next stanza, "*does not hurt / But makes me glad to think / That you might harbor love as well*" (16–18). Such mini-reversals, sleights of the lyric hand, abound: she appears to welcome him with joy (19–20), but she also seems proud (22); if she requites his love and makes him joyful (52–5), such joy will only lead to pain (56). Love, in the end, is a quantum of contradictory realities, oppositions, and paradoxical truths.

32 *That one piece validates a garden's fruit*: If one piece is good, then all the garden's fruit will be good as well. Knowing that he cannot "*tell a hundredth part / Of all the love*" (27–8) he bears for his beloved, the poet-lover argues that she should understand that one part should stand for all.

53 *If this were snow, then it would seem like fire*: The paradoxical conception of love as a state of contraries, and especially as "icy fire," will find its fullest realization in the lyrics of Petrarch a century later. But, it should be noted, neither Giacomo nor Petrarch invented this conceit, which was a standard image in love poetry.

13
My lady, I send you
Canzonetta of seven stanzas *singulars*, eight verses each:
abab cddc

This lyric uses verses of seven syllables each (*settenari*), making it a *canzonetta*, as also exemplified by *Extraordinarily* (2) and *I sing a sweet preamble* (17).

9–10 *You are so noble and so great / I love you always full of fear*: His fear derives from his love of a woman of high nobility ("alta" = high, in the sense of both class and morality).

19–20 *That every sigh could be / Alive and have a voice*: "Spirito" (spirit, soul), signifies the principle of life, the animating power, while "intelletto" (intellect) refers to the power of reason, which enables human beings to think and speak.

43 *When I portrayed your face*: Antonelli (296) rejects the meaning
"wax" for the word "cera" on the basis of phonetics. The word
derives from the Old French *chiere* (mod. *chère*), which becomes
"chere" in Middle English, "cheer" in Modern English. The archaic
sense of the word in English, "facial expression," lost its association
with face and came to mean simply an air or state of feeling, usually, though not necessarily, positive in connotation.

14

It's no surprise I grieve

Canzone of five stanzas *singulars*, seven octosyllabic verses each:
abab ccb

The lyric's theme, distant love ("amor lontano"), is modeled in part
on the troubador poet Jaufre Rudel's treatment in *Lanquan li jorn son
lonc e may*, the most celebrated example of the kind of love known
as "love from afar" (*amor de lonh*). Giacomo, however, describes the
experience of being separated from his beloved, whereas Jaufre's
expresses a love for a woman whom he has never seen, and, therefore,
distance from whom is an invention of the mind.

The lyric consists of five stanzas of seven verses, each of eight syllables, and stresses an interplay of opposites, the lady's beauty and
sweetness set against the poet's pain and suffering. What is remarkable
about the rhyme scheme is the *rima baciata* (rhyming couplet) of the
fifth and sixth verses of each stanza which express the theme of
presence/distance and capture a set of oppositions rhetorically: 5–6,
diviso – viso, deprivation – face (presence); 12–13, *allegranza / pesanza*,
happiness – pain; 19–20, *core – fore*, heart (inside) – outside; 26–7, *affare
– stare*, plight – dwell, i.e., the painful relationship versus the desire
and joy of being near the lady. The final stanza departs from this
oxymoronic pattern, stressing instead the lady's positive qualities, in
an example of *rima ricca* (rhyming of multiple syllables in sequence):
ornamento – parlamento, charm – (sweet) speech.

Interestingly, Giacomo's and Jaufre's lyrics share the same number
of verses per stanza (7), the same rhyme scheme, as well as number of
syllables per verse (8), although the number of stanzas differs (5 vs. 7).

16

Since neither mercy nor performing deeds
Canzone of five stanzas *unissonans*, nine verses each;
strict *capfinidas* resulting in an internal rhyme in each stanza except the first:
ABc ABc (c$_3$)D(d$_5$)BC

This lyric expresses all the conventions of the faithful yet long-sorrowing
lover, but the crux of his grief falls on the lady's erroneous belief that
he has been disloyal in taking on another lady's love, causing her to
revoke the pledge of love she had accorded him earlier. He proclaims
his innocence, but her piercing "smiling eyes" have the last word.

17

I sing a sweet preamble
Canzonetta of four stanzas, ten verses each;
the *fronte* remains the same while the *sirma* varies:
abab ccb ddb; ~ ccb ccb; ~ aac ddc; ~ bba bba

The sequence of *settenari* contributes an air of informality and simplicity
of spirit. Such a form is ideal for expressing clear and straightforward
thoughts uncomplicated by deep reflection or intricacy of reasoning, as
well as emotions characterized by a lack of conflict or irresolution. Here
joy and confidence prevail, the only threatening prospects to overshad-
ow the lovers' happiness being the possible appearance of a slanderer
and her husband's jealousy. But even these menaces are easily thwarted
by the lady's promise of fidelity to her lover, her witty dismissal of any
slanderer's possible affront, and her mocking criticism of her husband,
whose sexual limitations make him unable to satisfy his wife.

   4 *Agri*: most likely a reference to a river near Policoro, where
      Giacomo resided for a time.

   6 "*O star that shines so bright*": The reference is to the planet Venus,
      which can be seen in the early morning. In the Middle Ages the
      word "stella" signified either planet or star.

   11 "*Sweet lord*": The entire second stanza is devoted to the lady's reply
      to her lover's address, as are lines 28 to the end of the lyric, in
      which she reinforces her commitment to her lover. Nevertheless,
      it is possible to read the dialogue between the lover and lady dif-
      ferently, with the poet-lover speaking in verses 18–20 and 31–4,
      the lady in verses 11–17 and 35–40.

33 *Slanderer.* The "lusingatore," who seeks to besmirch the lover's reputation, is a stock figure in Occitan love poetry. The "salvaggio," verse 36, very likely refers to the lady's husband, who by tradition was considered to be lacking in courtly virtue. The word signifies the very opposite of "cortese."

40 *He's cold in summer too.* The word "gelore" signifies "coldness" (suggesting impotence or a lack of sexual appeal) and has a cognate in the word "gelidness." The Italian form plays on the word "geloso" ("jealous"), which evokes the topos of the *gilos,* the jealous husband whose sexual inadequacy causes him to fear being cuckolded.

18a
O god of Love, pray hear my plea
ABAB ABAB CDC DCD

This and the following four sonnets comprise a tenzone, or debate, between the Abbot of Tivoli and Giacomo on the topic of the nature of love, initiated by the Abbot.

1 *god of Love.* The persona appeals to the traditional pagan figure of Cupid who inspires the poet-lover, the figure in turn being associated with the Christian God in the image of "beard and hair."

6 *And sit with four snakes at all times.* The meaning of this image is uncertain and has generated a number of interpretations, none entirely convincing. Some critics regard the snakes as a metaphor for the four "thrones of Love," others as comprising an allusion to the snake in the book of Genesis and Eve (though without an explanation for the number four).

7 *On wings I travel far with ease.* The image refers to Cupid's wings.

9 *I have ascended all four steps.* Another obscure reference, possibly to the four steps leading to Cupid's palace, as Langley suggested (118). Antonelli (361), commenting on a reading by R. Schnell, contends the four steps refer to four of the five "punti d'amore" (elements of love) – namely, look, word, touch, and kiss – omitting the fifth, sexual gratification. He adds that the image may also have a parallel in mystic texts such as Richard of St Victor's *De quatuor*

gradibus violentae caritatis (The Four Steps of Violent Charity), or
Bernard de Clairvaux's *De diligendo Deo* (On Loving God).

13 *With your lead dart you've done the same.* According to mythology,
Cupid's golden arrows inspired love, the leaden arrows hatred.
The poet-lover is inspired to love, but his lady rejects his love
despite the fact that he has ascended to the status of being a
worthy lover.

18b
I have been wounded differently
ABAB ABAB CDE CDE

Giacomo rejects the Abbot's contention that love "contains divinity,"
hence his being "wounded differently" by love.

10 *I'll demonstrate just how and why.* the poet ironically adopts the very
terminology of the theologians – "io li lo mostreria per *quia* e quan-
ta" – in claiming to be able to argue like a theologian, while adding
that it would be a waste of his time. The Latin expression "*quia*,"
a formal term of Scholastic logic, served to refer to the method
of deductive reasoning used in proving the existence of God; the
word "quanto" was used in demonstrating the unity of God.

18c
One who rebukes another frequently
ABAB ABAB CDE CDE

The Abbot responds by asserting that Giacomo's love is shallow, which
makes him a spectator in matters of love and one whose critiques of
others therefore lack validity.

14 *Who lifts his arm hurts more than he who beats.* The one who lifts his
arm to defend himself feels the blows more than does the one
whose arm delivers them.

18d
A game like this has not been seen
ABAB ABAB CDC DCD

Giacomo adopts a cagey persona in his response to the Abbot's second lyric, suggesting he could speak out but that others would not believe him, and fearing he would be shamed and dishonored. But he does speak out, attacking those who stylize their love rhetorically and swear they will die unless saved by their lady love. He distances himself from the crowd of mediocre poets by presenting himself as more original and inventive: *For I abound with thoughts of love / That enter me as water does a sponge.*

   1 *A game like this has not been seen*: The game would seem to be the very exchange of the lyrics making up the tenzone itself.

18e
To honor you I send you this appeal
ABAB ABAB CDE CDE

The Abbot's response to Giacomo's previous lyric appears entirely sincere in its newfound praise for the poet, which would seem to derive from Giacomo's using somewhat humbler, more restrained, and less sarcastic language to criticize other poets.

19a
To stimulate my intellect
ABAB ABAB CAD CAD

Iacopo Mostacci initiates a tenzone with Pier della Vigna and Giacomo da Lentini concerning whether love, which is invisible, can be said to exist, that is, possess the quality of a substance. A member of the Sicilian School like Giacomo, Iacopo is the author of four canzoni, and he served as emperor Frederick II's official falconer.

19b
Because Love is not visible
ABAB ABAB CDB CDB

Pier della Vigna argues, in response to Iacopo's query, that despite the fact that love is invisible its power to rule the heart is sufficient proof that it exists. Pier served in the imperial court of Frederick II as chancellor and secretary, as well as jurist and diplomat. Imprisoned on false charges of offending the dignity of the emperor, he committed suicide, a sin for which Dante relegates him to the seventh circle of Hell among those who took their own lives (*Inferno* 13). Two of his canzoni, together with this sonnet, are extant.

> 13 *that love exists* ("ch'Amore sia"): In medieval Scholastic terms, the verb "to be" means "to exist as a substance," to be in the sense of having a physical existence that exists in and of itself, and that has the power to exist by itself independently of any other substance. Pier's conception means that love is a substance in the same way a stone is a substance, although it is not visible to the eye.

19c
Love's a desire that issues from the heart
ABAB ABAB ACD ACD

One of Giacomo's most celebrated lyrics, this sonnet offers a definition of the nature of love and provides a theoretical model that will become a standard for succeeding poets.

> 1 *Love's a desire that issues from the heart*: The word "disio" qualifies love as a passion, and as such it is therefore not a substance that exists independently of a material object. In medieval Scholastic terms, the passions are classified as "accidents," i.e., occurrences or events that take place in substances. The heart was considered the repository of all vital spirits that produce the passions in an individual, a concept derived from Aristotle's principles of the human anatomy.

> 14 *rules the world*: Giacomo stresses the universality of love, ending his sonnet with the same phrase as Pier, "fra la gente," forging an equivalence that ironically hides a difference. Giacomo seems to suggest that while he and Pier seek to define the nature of the same reality, namely love, his conception differs fundamentally, indeed radically, from Pier's.

20

The lily fades as soon as it is picked
ABAB ABAB CDE CDE

One of three sonnets whose rhyme pattern features equivocal words
(the same rhyme word with different meanings): *passo* and *giunta* in
the octave (a b a b, a b a b), and *punto, gente,* and *parte* (c d e, c d e)
in the sestet, with *punto* (c) forging a near rhyme with *giunta* (b).
The pattern, which exhibits Giacomo's exceptional rhetorical skill
as a poet, accentuates sameness within difference, a motif that cha-
racterizes, in some ways ironically, the nature of the poet amatory
experience. In the octave his experience mimes that of the analogue
– lover-lily, lover-prey, joined-disjoined – as the two quatrains lay the
stress on separation. The sestet, however, inversely stresses the poet-
lover's pledge never to part from his lady, uniformity and consistency
over diversity and change.

> 9–10 *Unhappy me, born at a point in time / When I could love but you, most
> noble one.* Born at an astrologically unpropitious time, the poet is
> a prisoner of destiny, seized by the ineluctable love of a lady that
> brings as much pain as joy.

21

Just like the sun that sends its rays
ABAB ABAB CDE CDE

As in the previous sonnet, equivocal or near rhymes abound: *spera*
(a: 1, 3, 5, 7) and *parte* (b: 2, 4, 6, 8), a rhyme word that *pare* (e: 11, 14)
closely parallels by sharing the same first syllable. They suggest likeness
and equality within difference, the prime *leitmotif* of the lyric, two
lovers whose love makes them one: *And it joins two hearts into one /
And teaches them the art of love: / Each loves the other equally* (12–14).

> 13 *The art of love.* The phrase "l'arte de l'amore" explicitly recalls the
> title of Ovid's *Ars amatoria* and Andreas Capellanus's *De arte honeste
> amandi.* Ovidian imagery pervades the sonnet.

22
How can so great a lady pass
ABAB ABAB CDC DCD

The sonnet entertains a *quaestio*, a philosophical query, concerning
the physical manner by which a seen object enters the mind of the
observer. The question may seem absurd to the modern reader, but
it received serious treatment by medieval thinkers.

   14 *The likeness of her mortal being:* The verse echoes the same concept
      Giacomo presented in his *canzonetta* "Meravigliosa-mente": *For in
      my heart I bear / The image of your form* (8–9).

23
Many lovers bear their malady
ABAB ABAB CDE CDE

The conception of love as a sickness or disease, known as *amor heros* or
amor hereos – from a scribal error for *eros* – was traditional in courtly
literature of the Middle Ages. It had its origin in Constantine of Africa's
Viaticum (before 1100), a text that adapted a medical handbook written
in the tenth century by an Arab physician.

24
My lady, your expressions raised in me
ABAB ABAB (b$_5$)CDE CDE

   7 *And you have seldom put to use your sail:* Critics are divided on the
     meaning of Giacomo's nautical metaphor. Some read the word
     "caro" as "carro," which refers to the lower part of a lateen sail
     (a triangular sail set on a long sloping spar), "penna" denoting
     the upper part of that sail. The phrase would then mean that the
     lady had reversed the positioning of the two, hence changed her
     habitual practice. I have, however, followed Antonelli's preferred
     reading, which takes "caro" to mean scarcity of use, or rare use
     (444), suggesting that the lady makes little effort to help the lover
     realize his aspirations.

25

A lover must protect his name
ABA(c$_5$)B ABA(c$_5$)B CDC DCD

The octave introduces a series of aphorisms promoting behaviour that all lovers should emulate, according to the poet-lover who, in the sestet, addresses his lady and declares that he will conduct himself with reserve in her presence so as to protect her against those who might wish to engage in false flattery, rumormongering, or slander. In Occitan poetry they are the *lausengiers*, and they have the power to destroy love.

> 6 *Since what is said can't be unsaid*: This familiar saying – "la parola non pò ritornare" – translates Horace's phrase "nescit vox missa reverti" (*Ars poetica*, 390).

26

On clear days I have seen it rain
ABAB ABAB (b$_5$)CDE CDE

This sonnet exemplifies Giacomo's rhetorical exploitation of paradox in presenting a series of apparent contradictions that characterize the illogical and ambiguous nature of love.

> 4 *And frozen snow engender heat*: The Italian adjective "freda" means "freezing," but in this context it must signify "frozen," since "frozen snow" or ice refers to crystal (crystallized quartz), which is glass that resembles ice. As a kind of glass it would have the power to reflect light like a lens and thereby create heat.

27

I've set my heart on serving God
ABAB ABAB CDC DCD

Giacomo's most well known and oft-cited lyric, whose association of love with paradise and the poet-lover's desire to reside there with his beloved prepares the way for Guinizzelli's and Dante's treatments of the topos.

> 14 *To see my love in glory's realm*: The word "glory" (*ghiora*) invariably signifies a condition of the afterlife in medieval literature and the essence of God in particular. Dante will open his *Paradiso* with it, placing it at the very beginning of the first verse: "La gloria di Colui che tutto move" (The glory of the One who moves all things). God, in essence, is glory, which is light.

28

Her face suffuses me with joy

$(c_3)A(c_5)B(c_3)A(c_5)B(c_3) A(c_5)B(c_5)A(c_5c)B$ CDC DCD

The sonnet exploits an internal rhyme pattern based on the word "viso," which appears toward the beginning of each verse of the octave and recurs as the rhyme word in the first verse of the sestet. The repetition seems designed to express the variety of the poet-lover's emotional responses to seeing his lady's face, which culminates in his seeming to visit paradise.

29

I see, but only from afar, her face

$(a_3a)A(a_5)B(a_3a)A(a_5)B (a_3a)AB(a_2)AB (a_3a)A(b_8)AB$ (a)AAB

Giacomo's rhetorical and metrical *tour de force* presenting a set of variations on the equivocality of the word "viso," creating a complex matrix of internal and end rhymes with the words "diviso" and "peraviso" (paradiso). The importance of the imagination as a power with the ability to retain the image of the beloved's appearance (here her face) and to activate an internal experience that removes the poet-lover to paradise is paramount in this lyric. We are here virtually at the threshold of the *Vita nuova*, in which Dante celebrates his love of Beatrice as a vehicle for attaining divine love, and of the *Commedia* as well: "*To see her face puts me in paradise, / And that is but to contemplate our Lord*" (7–8). Dante's conception of love is, of course, far more complex than Giacomo's, for whom the beloved is not a Christ figure possessing the power to save the poet-lover's soul, nor one who inspires him to continue his love of her after she dies.

30

A love so noble seized my heart

ABAB ABAB CDE CDE

The sonnet treats the traditional theme of the lady's arrogance ("altezze") and stoniness ("durezze"), which it inherited from the troubadours. These two terms, like others with a similar ending (e.g., "bellezze"), are singular in form, not plural, as is always the case in Giacomo's lyrics. The *bird of prey* ("aguila") to which the lady is compared is the eagle.

31

Through patience great success is won
ABAB ABAB CDE CDE

The poet takes comfort in the example of Job, whose faith in God is tested by a series of personal calamities, which, however, he succeeds in overcoming by virtue of his remarkable patience. By remaining patient during his suffering, Giacomo hopes to be rewarded by good fortune and granted relief, as was Job. This biblical example is unique in Giacomo's poetry, but its invocation lies outside its religious provenance. Job's story was simply the universal cultural touchstone for the virtue of patience during the Middle Ages.

32

It seems quite clear a noble lord should base
ABAB ABAB (a$_5$)CDC DCD

The lover's feeling of having been betrayed by the God of Love is a standard theme of Occitan poetry. The lyric contrasts the behaviour of the noble but harsh ruler ("bon signore") in the octave with that of Love in the sestet, which proceeds in precisely the opposite direction, from kindness to cruelty, and justifies the lover's accusation of treachery. The first stanza of the sestet is framed by the words "Amore" and "amaro," terms expressing antithesis whose similar sound and visual likeness suggest an underlying equivalence and become a standard oxymoron in love poetry.

33

Just as the butterfly in nature's grasp
A(a)BA(a)B A(a)BA(a)B CDE CDE

One of nine sonnets by Giacomo that feature internal rhymes – "natura – rancura" / "crëatura – cura" / "s'asigura – chiarura" / "l'arsura – ventura" – in the octave verses. The sestet reveals echoes of rhyme syllables: 9/10 "cor – mor," 12/13 "amor – ador(nezze)," and an equivocal use of the phrase "rendendo vita" in 11 (*giving up life*) vs. 13 (*giving life to*). The figures of speech express the dual and contrary nature of the singularity of love.

34

If one had never seen a flame of fire
(b₅)ABAB ABAB (b₅)CDE CDE

This is one of Giacomo's most copied sonnets, which suggests that it appealed to its early readers. It shares with the previous sonnet the image of love as a fiery passion that burns the lover, as well as the rhyme pattern ending in "–oco" in the octave.

35

No diamond, sapphire, emerald
ABAB ABAB CDC DCD

Compared with a variety of gems (nine in all), the poet-lover's lady excels all in beauty and power (*virtute*), equals the sun in splendor, and is more beautiful than the rose or any other flower. The pairing of the virtues "pregio ed onore" (worth and fame) was a standard phrase in troubadour poetry. The sonnet's octave is very compact in cataloguing the elements that make up the principal comparison. The heliotrope, also known as the bloodstone, was believed in the Middle Ages to have the power of rendering its holder invisible. As a whole the sonnet constitutes a poem of praise.

36

My lady's virtue and her worth
ABAB ABAB (b₅)CDC DCD

This sonnet of praise raises the bar to an extraordinary level of hyperbole in the final verses, as if the poet has run out of ways to describe his lady's worth, beauty, and peerlessness. So perfect is she that even God is hampered by her excellence, for though He could, He would choose not *to create someone just like her* ("che la potesse simile formare") if he had to create her over again. The lines can also be read to mean that God would not create someone else who might compete with the poet's lady, because her perfection does not admit of being exceeded. This "even God" motif will engage later poets of the amatory tradition, including, famously, Guinizzelli and Dante.

37

Angelic figure manifest

(f)A(a$_3$f)B(b)A(a$_3$a)B A(a$_3$)BA(a$_3$)B C(c$_4$)D(d$_5$)E C(c$_5$)D(d$_5$)E

This is the first lyric in Italian literature to equate the beloved with an angel, an analogy that Dante will develop in conceiving his beloved, Beatrice, a "donna-angelo," or "donna angelicata." The sonnet displays a complex degree of internal rhyme, and it represents, as mentioned earlier, one of only nine sonnets in which internal rhyme appears. The rhetorical feature is more commonly found in canzoni.

12 *And like your name, you wield the power.* The actual name of the lady has never been determined, though critics have advanced the names of Romana, Potenza, Comprobata, and also, of course, Angelica.

14 *As happens at the court of Rome.* The phrase "cità romana" could refer to Rome as the home of the Church or "papal court" (Santangelo, 1928) or as a homebase of the *Civitas Romana* or "imperial court" (Roncaglia, 1995). The references are from Antonelli's commentary in his 2008 edition of Giacomo's poems (547).

38

When someone has a true and loyal friend

ABAB ABAB CDE CDE

This sonnet, which treats the theme of friendship, is the only one of Giacomo's lyrics that does not concern the theme of love of woman, but rather morality. After the octave defines the nature of true friendship, the first half of the sestet takes up its antithesis in false friendship, only to repudiate its objectives and reaffirm the former's merits in the last half. The shift from true to false turns on the word "Ma" (but) in verse 9, and the word produces a similar effect at the same juncture in sonnet 32, *It seems quite clear a noble lord should base.* Giacomo characteristically juxtaposes the octave and sestet, setting up a structure that depends on a stated premise (protasis) followed by a response or effect (apodasis). At times this takes the form of presenting a universal truth followed by the poet-lover's personal response, as in sonnet 31, *Through patience great success is won,* in which the premise of Job's patience throughout his long adversity provides the basis of the poet's patient acceptance of his own suffering.

39
Remembering my loving fond farewell
Canzone of dubious authorship, five stanzas *singulars*, twelve verses each:
ABC ABC $c_5$dd$_5$ ee$_5$d

The first of three anonymous lyrics deemed of dubious attribution.
The strongest evidence that it is of the hand of Giacomo appears in the
third stanza, in which the poet persona speaks of being able to return
to Lentino in May.

40
Before a shiny mirror the basilisk
Sonnet of dubious authorship
ABAB ABAB CDE CDE

The basilisk was considered the king of the serpents by medieval
bestiaries. Like the basilisk, swan, peacock, and phoenix, the poet-
lover takes pleasure in his painful amatory experience which, after
destroying him, restores him to life by regenerating his amorous joy.

41
Looking at the deadly basilisk
Sonnet of dubious authorship
ABAB ABAB CDC DCD

As in the previous sonnet, several animals (the basilisk once again,
the asp, and the dragon) provide a template for comparison, not
with the poet-lover this time, but with the nature of love itself,
which is destructive and conducive only to pain. Unlike Giacomo's
other lyrics, this sonnet affords no positive element to balance the
negative, nor a final twist of logic in the closing verses. It is a lyric
in a single key with no modulation.

Bibliography

Editions of Giacomo da Lentini's Poetry

I poeti della Scuola siciliana. Vol. 1: *Giacomo da Lentini*. Ed. Roberto Antonelli. Milan: Mondadori, 2008.

Poeti italiani della corte di Federico II. Ed. Bruno Panvini. Naples: Liguori, 1994.

Giacomo da Lentini: Poesie. Ed. Roberto Antonelli. Rome: Bulzoni, 1979.

Le rime della scuola siciliana. Vol. 1. Ed. Bruno Panvini. Florence: Olschki, 1962.

Poeti del Duecento. Vol. 1. Ed. Gianfranco Contini. Milan: Riccardo Ricciardi, 1960.

The Poetry of Giacomo da Lentino, Sicilian Poet of the Thirteenth Century. Ed. Ernest Langley. Cambridge, Mass.: Harvard University Press, 1915.

Other Primary Texts Cited

Bonagiunta Orbicciani da Lucca. *Rime*. Ed. Aldo Menichetti. Florence: SISMEL, 2012.

Chiaro Davanzati. *Canzoni e sonetti*. Ed. Aldo Menichetti. Turin: Einaudi, 2004.

Folquet de Marselha. *Poesie*. Ed. Paolo Squillacioti. Rome: Carocci, 2003.

Guittone d'Arezzo. *Selected Poetry and Prose*. Trans. Antonello Borra. Toronto: University of Toronto Press, 2017.

Perdigó, Luisa Marina. *The Life, Poetry, and Music of the Provençal Troubadour Perdigon: Texts, Translations, and Interpretations*. New York: Edwin Mellen Press, 2013.

The Poems of the Troubadour Bertran de Born. Ed. and trans. William D. Paden Jr, Tilde Sankovitch, and Patricia H. Stäblein. Berkeley: University of California Press, 1986.

The Poetry of the Sicilian School. Ed. and trans. Frede Jensen. New York: Garland, 1986.

The Poetry of Cercamon and Jaufre Rudel. Ed. George Wolf and Roy Rosenstein. Garland Library of Medieval Literature, 5. New York: Garland, 1983.

Criticism

Abulafia, David. *Frederick II: A Medieval Emperor.* Oxford: Oxford University Press, 1988.

Antologia della poesia italiana: Duecento. Ed. Cesare Segre and Carlo Ossola. Turin: Einaudi, 1999.

Antonelli, Roberto. "Giacomo da Lentini e l'invenzione della lirica italiana." *Critica del testo* 12.1 (2009): 1–24.

– "Dal Notaro a Guinizzelli." In *Da Guido Guinizzelli a Dante. Nuove prospettive sulla lirica del Duecento,* Atti del Convegno di studi (Padova-Monselice, 10–12 maggio 2002), ed. F. Brugnolo and G. Peron, 107–46. Padova, 2004.

Barolini, Teodolinda. "Dante and the lyric past." In *The Cambridge Companion to Dante.* Ed. Rachel Jacoff, second ed. Cambridge, UK: Cambridge University Press, 2007.

Brugnolo, Furio. "I siciliani e l'arte dell'imitazione: Giacomo da Lentini, Rinaldo d'Aquino e Iacopo Mostacci 'traduttori' dal provenzale." *La parola del testo* 3 (1999): 45–74.

I canzonieri della lirica italiana delle Origini. 4 vols. Ed. Lino Leonardi. Florence: SISMEL Edizioni del Galuzzo, 2001.

Coluccia, Rosario. *Storia, lingua e filologia della poesia antica: Scuola siciliana, Dante e altro.* Florence: Franco Cesati, 2016.

Cornish, Alison. *Vernacular Translation in Dante's Italy: Illiterate Literature.* Cambridge, UK: Cambridge University Press, 2011.

Crespo, Roberto. "Lettura del sonetto *Chi non avesse mai veduto foco* di Giacomo da Lentini." *Medioevo romanzo* 12 (1987): 353–62.

Damiani, Rolando. "La replicazione del viso amato in due sonetti di Giacomo da Lentini." In *Miscellanea di studi in onore di Vittore Branca,* 1:79–93. Florence: Olschki, 1980.

Dante's De vulgari eloquentia. Ed. and trans. Steven Botterill. Cambridge, UK: Cambridge University Press, 1996.

Delle Donne, Fulvio. *Federico II: la condanna della memoria: metamorfosi di un mito.* Rome: Viella, 2012.

Folena, Gianfranco. "Cultura e poesia dei Siciliani." In *Storia della letteratura italiana.* Ed. Emilio Cecchi and Natalino Sapegno, 1: 273–347. Milan: Garzanti, 1965.

– *Volgarizzare e tradurre.* Turin: Einaudi, 1991.

Federico II e le nuove culture: Atti del XXXI Convegno storico internazionale. Spoleto: Centro italiano di studi sull'alto Medioevo, 1995.

Fratta, Aniello. *Le fonti provenzali dei poeti della scuola siciliana: i postillati del Torraca e altri contributi.* Florence: Le Lettere, 1996.

Intellectual Life at the Court of Frederick II Hohenstaufen. Ed. William Tronzo. Washington, DC: National Gallery of Art, 1994.

Kleinhenz, Christopher. "Giacomo da Lentini and Dante: The Early Italian Sonnet Tradition in Perspective." *The Journal of Medieval and Renaissance Studies* 8 (1978): 217–34.

– *The Early Italian Sonnet: The First Century (1220–1321).* Lecce: Milella, 1986.

The Making of the Sonnet. Ed. Edward Hirsch and Eavan Boland. New York: Norton, 2008.

Mallette, Karla. *The Kingdom of Sicily, 1100–1250: A Literary History.* Philadelphia: University of Pennsylvania Press, 2005.

Marti, Mario. "Iacopo da Lentini." *Enciclopedia dantesca*, 3: 334–6.

Morpurgo, Piero. "*Philosophia naturalis* at the Court of Frederick II: From the Theological Method to the *ratio secundum physicam.*" In *Intellectual Life at the Court of Frederick II Hohenstaufen*, ed. William Tronzo, 241–50. Washington, DC: National Gallery of Art, 1994.

Picone, Michelangelo. *Percorsi della lirica duecentesca: dai Siciliani alla* Vita nova. Florence: Cadmo, 2003.

La poesia di Giacomo da Lentini: Scienza e filosofia nel XIII secolo in Sicilia e nel Mediterraneo occidentale. Ed. Rossend Arqués. Palermo: Centro di studi filologici e linguistici siciliani, 2000.

Pötters, Wilhelm. *Nascita del sonetto. Metrica e matematica al tempo di Federico II.* Ravenna: Longo, 1998.

Quaglio, Antonio Enzo. "I poeti della 'Magna Curia' siciliana." In *La letteratura italiana: storia e testi*, ed. Carlo Muscetta, 1/1: 171–240. Bari: Laterza, 1970.

Rashed, Roshdi. "Fibonacci et les mathématiques arabes." In *Le scienze alla corte di Federico II*, ed. Véronique Pasche. Paris: Brepols, 1994.

Roncaglia, Aurelio. "De quibusdam provincialibus translatis in lingua nostra." In *Letteratura e critica: studi in onore di Natalino Sapegno*, 2: 1–36. Rome: Bulzoni, 1975.

– "Angelica figura." *Cultura neolatina* 55 (1995): 4–65.

Rossetti, Dante Gabriel. *The Early Italian Poets.* Ed. Sally Purcell. Berkeley: University of California Press, 1981.

Russell, Rinaldina. "Giacomo da Lentini e l'anti-canzone: note sul discordo italiano." *Modern Philology* 77/3 (1977): 297–304.

Santangelo, Salvatore. *Il volgare illustre e la poesia siciliana del secolo XIII.* Palermo, 1923.

– *Le tenzoni poetiche nella letteratura italiana delle origini.* Geneva: Olschki, 1928.

Schiaffini, Alfredo. *Momenti di storia della lingua italiana*, second ed. Rome: Leonardo da Vinci, 1953.

Schnell, Rüdiger. *Causa amoris. Liebeskonzeption und Liebesdarstellung in der mittelalterlichen Literatur.* Bern: Francke, 1985.

Sciascia, Laura. "Lentini e i Lentini dai Normanni al Vespro." In *La poesia di Giacomo da Lentini: Scienza e filosofia nel XIII secolo in Sicilia e nel Mediterraneo occidentale,* ed. Rossend Arqués, 18–23. Palermo: Centro di studi filologici e linguistici siciliani, 2000.

Tonelli, Natascia. "De Guidone de Cavalcantibus physico (con una noterella su Giacomo da Lentini ottico)." In *Per Domenico De Robertis: Studi offerti dagli allievi fiorentini,* 459–508. Ed. Isabella Becherucci et al. Florence: Le Lettere, 2000.

Torraca, Francesco. "A proposito di Folchetto." In *Nuovi studi danteschi,* 479–502. Naples: Federico e Ardia, 1921.

– *Studi su la lirica italiana del Duecento.* Bologna: Zanichelli, 1902.

Vanasco, Rocco. *La poesia di Giacomo da Lentini. Analisi strutturali.* Bologna: Pátron, 1979.

Index of First Lines

Index of Names

THE LORENZO DA PONTE ITALIAN LIBRARY

General Editors: Luigi Ballerinia and Massimo Ciavolella

Pellegrino Artusi, *Science in the Kitchen and the Art of Eating Well* (2003).
Edited and translated by Luigi Ballerini and Murtha Baca
Lauro Martines, *An Italian Renaissance Sextet: Six Tales in Historical
Context* (2004). Translated by Murtha Baca
Aretino's Dialogues (2005). Translated by Margaret Rosenthal and
Raymond Rosenthal
Aldo Palazzeschi, *A Tournament of Misfits: Tall Tales and Short* (2005).
Translated by Nicolas J. Perella
Carlo Cattaneo, *Civilization and Democracy: The Salvemini Anthology of
Cattaneo's Writings* (2006). Edited and introduced by Carlo G. Lacaita
and Filippo Sabetti. Translated by David Gibbons
Benedetto Croce, *Breviary of Aesthetics: Four Lectures* (2007). Translated
by Hiroko Fudemoto, Introduction by Remo Bodei
Antonio Pigafetta, *First Voyage around the World (1519–1522): An Account
of Magellan's Expedition* (2007). Edited and translated by Theodore J.
Cachey Jr.
Raffaello Borghini, *Il Riposo* (2008). Translated by Lloyd H. Ellis Jr.
Paolo Mantegazza, *Physiology of Love and Other Writings* (2008). Edited
and translated by Nicoletta Pireddu
Renaissance Comedy: The Italian Masters (2008). Edited and translated by
Donald Beecher
Cesare Beccaria, *On Crimes and Punishments and Other Writings* (2008).
Edited by Aaron Thomas; Translated by Aaron Thomas and Jeremy
Parzen; Foreword by Bryan Stevenson; Introduction by Alberto Burgio
Leone Ebreo, *Dialogues of Love* (2009). Edited and translated by Cosmos
Damian Bacich and Rossella Pescatori
Boccaccio's Expositions on Dante's Comedy (2009). Translated by Michael
Papio
My Muse Will Have a Story to Paint: Selected Prose of Ludovico Ariosto
(2010). Translated with an Introduction by Dennis Looney
*The Opera of Bartolomeo Scappi (1570): L'arte et prudenza d'un maestro
Cuoco (The Art and Craft of a Master Cook)* (2011). Translated with
commentary by Terence Scully
Pirandello's Theatre of Living Masks: New Translations of Six Major Plays
(2011). Translated by Umberto Mariani and Alice Gladstone Mariani

From Kant to Croce: Modern Philosophy in Italy, 1800–1950 (2012). Edited and translated with an introduction by Brian P. Copenhaver and Rebecca Copenhaver

Giovan Francesco Straparola, *The Pleasant Nights,* Volume 2 (2012). Edited with an Introduction by Donald Beecher

Giovan Francesco Straparola, *The Pleasant Nights,* Volume 1 (2012). Edited with an Introduction by Donald Beecher

Giovanni Botero, *On the Causes of the Greatness and Magnificence of Cities* (2012). Translated and with an introduction by Geoffrey W. Symcox

John Florio, *A Worlde of Wordes* (2013). A Critical Edition with an Introduction by Hermann W. Haller

Giordano Bruno, *On the Heroic Frenzies* (2013). A Translation of *De gli eroici furori* by Ingrid D. Rowland; Text edited by Eugenio Canone

Alvise Cornaro, *Writings on the Sober Life: The Art and Grace of Living Long* (2014). Translated by Hiroko Fudemoto; Introduction by Marisa Milani; Foreword by Greg Critser

Dante Alighieri, *Dante's Lyric Poetry: Poems of Youth and of the Vita Nuova.* (2014). Edited, with a general introduction and introductory essays by Teodolinda Barolini. With new verse translations by Richard Lansing. Commentary translated into English by Andrew Frisardi

Vincenzo Cuoco, *Historical Essay on the Neapolitan Revolution of 1799* (2014). Edited and Introduced by Bruce Haddock and Filippo Sabetti. Translated by David Gibbons

Vittore Branca, *Merchant Writers: Florentine Memoirs from the Middle Ages and Renaissance* (2015). Translated by Murtha Baca

Carlo Goldoni, *Five Comedies* (2016). Edited by Michael Hackett and Gianluca Rizzo. With an Introduction by Michael Hackett and an essay by Cesare De Michelis

Those Who from Afar Look like Flies: An Anthology of Italian Poetry from Officina to the Present (2016). Edited by Luigi Ballerini and Beppe Cavatorta. With a Foreword by Marjorie Perloff

Guittone d'Arezzo, *Selected Poems and Prose* (2017). Selected, translated, and with an introduction by Antonello Borra

Giordano Bruno, *The Ash Wednesday Supper* (2018). A new translation of *La Cena de le Ceneri* with the Italian text annotated and introduced by Hilary Gatti

Remo Bodei, *Geometry of the Passions: Fear, Hope, Happiness: Philosophy and Political Use* (2018). Translated by Gianpiero W. Doebler

Scipio Sighele, *The Criminal Crowd and Other Writings on Mass Society* (2018). Edited, with an Introduction and Notes, by Nicoletta Pireddu. Translated by Nicoletta Pireddu and Andrew Robbins. With a Foreword by Tom Huhn

Giacomo da Lentini, *The Complete Poems* (2018). Translated and annotated by Richard Lansing. Introduction by Akash Kumar